MIRROR
by the
ROAD

*For Getting So Quickly
To The HEART Of The Matter.
With Love & Best Wishes,
Peter
11-27-04*

MIRROR by the *ROAD*

A Transforming Journey
of Spirituality in Everyday Life

Peter Oppenheimer

Inner Wealth Press
P.O. Box 487
Forest Knolls, California 94933

Grateful acknowledgement is made to the following publishers for granting permission to reprint portions of the listed publications: Princeton University Press for a passage from *The I Ching or Book of Changes* translated by Richard Wilhelm and rendered into English by Cary F. Baynes, copyright 1950 and renewed 1977; Yale University Press for a passage from *Psychology and Religion* by Carl Jung, copyright 1938; Doubleday & Company for passages from *The I Ching Workbook* by R.L. Wing, copyright 1979; and Chetana Publishers in Bombay for a passage from *I am That*, talks with Sri Nisargadatta Maharaj translated by Maurice Frydman, copyright 1982.

Copyright ©1988 by Peter Oppenheimer
All rights reserved.

First Edition

Library of Congress Catalog Card Number 88-80780
ISBN 0-945925-03-4
Cataloging-in-Publication Data Available Upon Request

---

88 89 90 91 92 BCI 10 9 8 7 6 5 4 3 2 1

cover illustration by Carl Dennis Buell
cover and interior design by Stephanie Jurs
photo insert design by Stephanie Furniss
printed by BookCrafters Inc. in the United States of America

This book is dedicated
to the numerous friends and families in India
who showered me with their love
and to their culture which reveals that the source of all love
shines as the core of each self.

This book is also dedicated
with loving gratitude to each reader.
In some mysterious way your aspirations and potentials
are at once its cause and its effect.

Contents

	Acknowledgments	ix
	Preface	xi
1.	Before The Beginning	1
2.	The Quality of Rice & The Quality of Life	4
3.	Three Steps	8
4.	Close Enough To Pretend	13
5.	Garbage in Paradise	16
6.	Three Strikes And You're In	19
7.	Time Flies (Coach Class)	22
8.	The Indian Honeymooners	28
9.	Singapore's Veneer	31
10.	A Passing Shadow	34
11.	Benign Chaos	37
12.	A City Awakens	39
13.	Reinitiations	42
14.	The Empty Boat	47
15.	Rejoining The Guru	50
16.	Man At Leisure/God At Work	55
17.	The Road To Malayatoor	62

18.	Wealth Beyond Money	65
19.	The World In The Self	69
20.	Like Rays Of Sun	74
21.	When Heaven Goes To Hell	79
22.	The Luxury Of Simplicity	82
23.	An Atheist Goes To Temple	88
24.	The Land Of Prince	91
25.	In The Garden Of Faith	95
26.	Inaugural Address	101
27.	The Presence And Presents Of The Guru	107
28.	The Extended Self & Its Intended "Other"	111
29.	Swept Away	118
30.	Dancing Gods On The Malabar Coast	120
31.	Inaction In Action	125
32.	Killer Pain And Pain Killer	133
33.	The Secret Of Devotion	137
34.	From The Excruciating To The Exquisite	141
35.	One Indian Family	146
36.	Yoga As Consolation Prize	152
37.	Fluctuations Of Joy	156
38.	Waning With The Moon	161
39.	Life And Death Valley	164
40.	The Benevolent Dictator	168
41.	Leave Takings – I	174
42.	Leave Takings – II	180
43.	The End As Beginning	184

Acknowledgments

A book is like a baby—lots of fun to conceive but very painful to deliver. This particular book has had countless midwives and midhusbands. As the book itself demonstrates, I am immensely indebted to Nitya Chaitanya Yati, my spiritual teacher and undeclared therapist, who over the years has mysteriously transformed into the most radiant core of my own consciousness.

Had it not been for the innocent gift of a blank journal from Stephen Dietz, it is not likely this project would have developed. During the long months of manuscript preparation and rewriting, I had the good fortune of access to the computer of Thomas Loudat, who allowed his study to become my bedroom and workshop.

When I was eager to rest content with an early draft, I was gently but firmly dissauded from such folly by my two wonderful editors, Wyn and Don Child. Their constructive criticism and provocative suggestions are responsible for the structure and focus of this present version. I want to issue a special thanks to my good friend, John Sausedo, whose frequent phone calls and occasional visits kept the solitude necessary for writing from turning into a sense of total isolation.

I am grateful to Stephanie Furniss, who in spite of all the demands of a baby and a business gave freely of her time and expertise to get me started in the conceptualizing of a book's design. My dear friend and mentor from Stanford,

Dr. Helen Schrader, is never far from my thoughts. Some of my best ideas are echoes of her wisdom.

Wendi Kallins and Lew Tremaine acted as guardian angels in opening their newspaper office and its computer for my use during final revisions. Barry Prince took time out of his busy schedule to give encouragement and guidance. Fortunately the readers will never know just how indebted they are to Brent MacKinnon and Carolyn Eden for their editorial genius. Their red pens have saved readers a lot of grief. Any awkwardness that remains is there in spite of their loving protests.

Roy Carlisle has meant more to me through the final stages of this project than he could probably imagine. It is hard to say which was more indispensible—his knowledge of the book industry, his sense of aesthetics, or his compassion. A special thanks is due Deborah Buchanan for providing the photograph which formed the basis for the cover illustration by Carl Buell. Steve and Jean Kinsey's warmth and humor have been a constant source of nourishment and support.

Finally, I would certainly be remiss if I did not acknowledge an abiding sense of gratitude to my mother. Once again she has proved herself willing to stand by me even when unsure of precisely "where I'm at." To these and all the many many people who have opened their hearts and homes to me, I bow my head and wish the very best.

Preface

When Alexander the Great first arrived in India with his conquering hordes, he immediately began to hear tales of *yogis*, great holy men who were said to have miraculous powers. Such stories threatened his vanity, for he felt himself to be the most powerful man alive. He felt that his unprecedented conquests proved this. In an irritated and skeptical state, he asked one of his lieutenants to locate and bring a yogi before him.

The next morning a scrawny looking man dressed in a loin cloth was ushered into the great conquerer's presence. There was something in the upright posture and penetrating gaze of the yogi that caused Alexander to suppress the mocking laughter that he felt well up in him at the thought that such a man could be considered his equal.

With a wave of his hand he silenced the sarcastic whisperings of his attendants and then addressed the yogi directly. "It seems that many of your countrymen are mightily impressed with the powers of you and some of your peers. Before I send my troops to take over your towns and villages, I first want to see what I am dealing with. Tonight you and your friends shall come before me and give us a demonstration of your powers."

The yogi was summarily dismissed. In the middle of the afternoon, word arrived for Alexander that the holy men had requested the preparation of a large bonfire for the evening's demonstration. Alexander ordered his servants to make the necessary arrangements.

That evening the courtyard outside of the conquerer's tent was abuzz with anticipation. At the appointed hour a dozen yogis showed up. Igniting the wood in the pit, they slowly and gracefully paraded three times around the fire. They paused, bowed to Alexander, and one of them spoke, "Oh Great Sir, may the sweet light of wisdom dawn within you. Unlike you, we cannot claim to have conquered over others, but what we have conquered is our own fear of death." Saying this, they bowed once more to the man who was to become known as "The Great," turned, bowed to the fire, peacefully entered its flames and were consumed.

Apparently Alexander was greatly impressed. The next morning he and all his soldiers broke camp and withdrew from India, the only place from which they were ever to do so.

It is not only in matters of war and peace, life and death, that Indian society turns inside-out Western notions of true and false, right and wrong. Another example can be seen in their topsy-turvey approach to matters of the sacred and the profane. In India stray cows (and even their dung) are afforded the reverence which in the West is reserved for the Pope. On the other hand Krishna, one of their most beloved deities, is celebrated as being a neighborhood thief during his childhood, and is glorified as a young man who was not beyond pilfering young ladies' undergarments while they were enjoying their bath.

For the Westerner, India bristles with contrasts, contradictions, and seeming irrationalities. In addition, India is brimming with natural beauty, architectural wonders and the milk of loving kindness. Humor and devoutness vie and mingle as the cornerstones of the Indian psyche. Visiting India can be an inspiring experience, at once dazzling one's senses, challenging one's mind, conquering one's heart, and stirring one's soul. This book is an invitation to taste such an experience and to reflect upon the personal and social transformations that it suggests.

Over the past fifteen years, I have visited India seven times and have lived there a total of three years. The journal of my most recent trip (November 1986 – February 1987) provides the skeleton for this book which is then fleshed out by flashbacks and reminiscences of earlier experiences and observations.

My first trip to India in 1971 unfolded against the personal backdrop of an identity crisis and the anxiety of an uncertain future. This most recent journey was undertaken in the midst of what I suppose could be called a "mid-life crisis." Over the years my exposure to and immersion in Indian culture has brought about personal transformations and has changed my relationship with the outer world.

Although the present story dramatizes these transformations, the experiences described and the lessons imbibed are meant to be suggestive rather than definitive. This book is intended to be your story too, as the mystery and earthiness of India begin to work a little of their magic on how you see yourself and experience your world.

It was common for me to meet people in India who were under the impression that most Americans are millionaires, carry guns and have been to the moon. I found that our preconceptions about India are often equally misguided. The stereotypes of poverty and squalor which correctly characterize certain urban pockets in India, as indeed in all major American cities too, had little relevance once one moved out into the rural areas. The misconception becomes even more dramatic given that eighty percent of the population in India is rural. (In America eighty percent of the population is urban and suburban.)

In rural India profound questions about the nature of "wealth" and "poverty" take on dimensions that are rarely considered in the West. Further, there is a vast middle class of Indians. Excluding them from the attempt to understand India would be similar to disregarding the existence of middle class Americans while trying to discover what makes our country tick. My experiences in India not only caused me to reevaluate wealth as it relates to India, but even more so I find that my own goals and appreciations regarding wealth have been turned inside out.

Another grave misconception about India that has arisen in the West has to do with the nature and function of a guru. Unscrupulous charlatans, gullible seekers and a sensationalistic media have each in their own way contributed to the vulgarization of a subtle spiritual dynamic which resides at the very heart of Indian culture. Guru literally means "that which dispels darkness." There is an inner darkness or ignorance which is said to be the cause of all bondage and suffering. Light, or true knowledge, leads to liberation and happiness. A guru functions as a mirror for a student's own inner resources of enlightenment. Ultimately each of us carries the guru-principle within ourself, and an outer guru is at best a reminder. Exactly how the guru-dynamic works is illuminated in the following pages.

Just as technology and material progress have been the guiding stars directing the evolution of our culture the past several hundred years, spirituality and self-knowledge have been the central values informing the culture of India for several thousands of years. The members of each culture can now greatly benefit from the fruits of each other's efforts. This book is an attempt to offer some of the fruit of Indian culture to be tasted, digested and utilized by Western readers.

The "pursuit of happiness" has from the very beginning been a hallmark of American life. Getting to the root of human suffering (in order to uproot it) has from the beginning been a hallmark of Indian life. Ironically in our pursuit of happiness, we seem to have generated a tangle of stress, disease, and dissatisfaction, as well as physical, emotional and environmental abuses of various sorts. Ironically in their search for the roots of suffering, the people of India have uncovered a base of self-founded peace and well-being that tends to translate outwardly as love and compassion.

The gift of India for a Westerner is that it embodies a universal message wrapped in an exotic package. The contents without the wrapping can seem etherial if not preposterous. The wrapping without the contents can seem chaotic if not "madness." Together they present an experience at once sensuous and mystical, aesthetic and transcendent. When the sights and insights of Indian life are combined, we get a peep into a world which sometimes seems like another planet and yet speaks to us with a significance that can enhance our own daily lives.

Exposure to India is a liberating experience, challenging habits and conventions previously taken for granted and illuminating new dimensions of oneself and ways of relating to others. It is my hope that this book reflects being in India as an adventure that engages one's body, senses, heart, mind and soul, after which the exotic seems customary and the familiar seems phenomenal.

Peter Oppenheimer
California
May 1988

1

Before The Beginning

Last night I was startled awake by a house-shaking, window-rattling, tree-splitting electrical storm. For an hour and a half the tumult held me spellbound in awe. My heart was thumping triple time as the sky flashed right into my room. The storm rumbled, roared, crackled and exploded with a volume and force unparalleled by any man-made activity (except the bomb).

It was a profoundly religious experience. On the one hand my body trembled, sensing its primordial vulnerability and dependence on the mercy of the forces of nature. On the other hand, my soul was gripped in solitary communion with the magnificent and formidable powers of the universe —powers which can create an entire galaxy and obliterate it with equal ease. It was thrilling to know with intuitive certainty that the very same power rumbling above also courses through our veins as the life-force. The majestic miracle of electricity momentarily turned darkest night into bright day, just as the magical radiance of consciousness illuminates inner and outer worlds of great fascination.

The storm, like everything else making up the phenomenal world, passed. In its wake the world seemed cleansed and refreshed. Those of us who had allowed ourselves to be touched by it were at once humbled and ennobled, calmed and inspired.

Thus in the calm between storms this journal finds its inception. For me the next storm is likely to be the apparent chaos that inevitably greets a Western visitor to the Indian subcontinent. For reasons that shall become evident, I have chosen India as the ideal crucible in which to cast myself for some much needed healing, regeneration and reorientation.

This morning I can sense my upcoming trip, indeed the rest of my life, as stretching before me with a mystery and promise that is mirrored in the blank pages of my empty journal. Emptiness is perhaps the greatest wealth one can possess, for it provides the arena for adventure, discovery and creativity.

In Western culture emptiness tends to be feared and avoided as poverty rather than appreciated and embraced as treasure. Every room is to be filled with objects, and every hour of every day has its pressing activity. Yet it is only the empty vessel that can be filled, and it is only in silence that one hears the soft still voice from within. This is why I have cultivated a personal aspiration to at least be "good for *nothing*," only after which do I care to be good for something.

Just as this empty journal is a loving and empowering gift given to me by a dear friend, so is this Vast Unknown into which I am today stepping, the greatest gift granted to each of us by the Unseen Giver. Hopefully as my upcoming journey proceeds through Hawaii, Singapore, India, and points unknown, and as I fill these perfectly blank pages with images, thoughts, observations and experiences, a bit of that regenerating blessedness of emptiness will still shine through and between the lines.

It seems fitting that the journal should commence in Winnetka, Illinois where I spent the first eighteen years of my life and where my mother continues to reside. Here from kindergarten, I attended Greeley School. Several times a day I passed under the image of the famous American, Horace Greeley, whose appeal, "Go west, young man, go west," set the tone for an entire nations's restless history. That itch to pursue the setting sun is still under the skin of many Americans, and California and Arizona may soon sink under the resultant weight. If one perseveres in moving west, in body and/or mind and spirit, one will eventually land in the East, the direction from which the rising sun is forever heralding brand new days.

The past twenty years have witnessed a tidal wave in the collective psyche of a generation of Westerners, lifting them to a great interest in Asian and Oriental culture, philosophy and religion. At the same time peoples of the East have been restlessly turning envious eyes westward at the technological advancement and material opulence of the West. Perhaps we are now on the brink of a synthesis in which the "twain" finally do meet to the mutual enrichment of all. On this journey and in this journal, I hope to explore and illustrate much of what the East has to offer to us in the West, whereby our "quality of life" can reach or surpass the level of our "standard of living."

During this brief visit back to Winnetka, the simple fact hit me like a revelation that no matter how far or where I journey in this lifetime, one thing that will remain constant is that this is where I am from. I don't know why that should feel reassuring or consoling, but on my several strolls this time along the lake, across rich green manicured lawns, under stately elms, oaks, and maple trees, it did. There is still a peaceful, almost timeless quality to the North Shore (of Lake Michigan), which in my college years rankled me as being isolated, sheltered and removed from the stinging social problems all around it.

In several previous visits to India I have noticed some dramatic contrasts and some surprising correspondences between life in a South Indian village and that in a North American suburb. This will undoubtedly also be one of the facets of this upcoming journey which commences in three days when, after tying up some loose ends in California where I have been living, I take off from San Francisco for Hawaii en route to Asia.

2

The Quality of Rice & The Quality of Life

It is now two days before my departure. I have just finished eating some rice which I cooked for my dinner. I truly relished it. I marvel at what seems to me an unbroken chain of miracles which has evoked these grains from the earth (mysteriously helped along by water, sun, and air) and then through an intricate matrix of much toil and unseen labor has brought them from the field to the barn to the distributor to the market to my pantry. Further, the unchewable indigestible grains, when put in water over fire, magically swell up and become soft and tasty. Even more mind-boggling is that I have a tongue equipped with certain taste buds which delightfully complement the grains of rice. Now, as I write this, without the slightest conscious effort on my part, those grains are being chemically broken down, re-cooked and prepared for transformation into a potential energy which can be used in any cell in my body for any activity in which I engage.

What has actually happened is "nothing more" than a mundane activity which I and most of my fellow human beings engage in tens of thousands of times in a normal lifetime. But tonight I tapped more joy out of each mouthful than I usually experience in an entire meal.

Was the quality of the rice extraordinary tonight?

I am certain that was not the case.

Then what was unique about this particular meal that lifted me to and through a sensual enchantment to an emotional sense of reverence, an intellectual appreciation of the workings of Nature, a psychic sense of communion with all creation, and ultimately elevated me to a sense of spiritual well-being?

The essential ingredient in all this is my own consciousness, my own awareness of the processes involved, my own vision of the Reality which appears to me to be coquettishly hiding behind and yet still shining through the world of appearance. I am indebted to the people with whom I have lived in India during several visits over the past fifteen years for teaching me the role which one's own consciousness plays in the quality of one's life.

An assumption behind my making this journey to India as well as my writing about it is, "To a great extent each of us is free to determine the texture and quality of our own life." One of my purposes in undertaking the journey is to right my own ship after a period of stagnation and a series of misfortunes. One of my purposes in writing this book is to present the reader with an experiential basis for understanding the life style, world view and spirituality of India which in turn can serve as a guide for self-reflection and ultimately the enhancement of the quality of one's own life.

Consciously or unconsciously we are always actively engaged in the creation of our own world of experience. In this regard my Indian teacher once compared life to a game of cards. The possibilities are, at the outset, limited by the number of cards in the deck. Similarly the nature of the cards we are dealt is determined by some Unseen Hand. Hence the possibilities and the probabilities are greatly beyond our conscious manipulation. But when it comes to actualizing a configuration of events out of the given potentialities, we are free to be as foolish or clever as we wish or have prepared ourself to be.

Out of the vast range of dreamy possibilities or ideas we carry with us, at any given moment we can only promote one of these to the realm of actuality. Different people at different levels of awareness will not play the same cards in the same way. Success or wisdom is determined by the extent to which we keep our values, ideals, and intentions as guiding lights so that in each moment we can promote an ideal into an actual.

Too often we are lulled to sleep by becoming immersed in or hypnotized by the presented set of stimuli or circumstances. In this way we are continually *reacting* to what has already been created rather than *acting* or creating what is still only an internal vision or a seed within our consciousness. Emphasis on the former naturally makes life seem predetermined, and we feel bound. Emphasis on the latter lifts our self-identity into the very fire of creation, and we feel free.

Matter is what has already been "determined," and Spirit is eternally the "determining" factor, keeping life ever fresh and new. Each human being is a wonderful blend of Spirit and Matter, with Mind as the common meeting ground.

For thousands of years the Indian culture has placed great emphasis on the Spirit and hence tended to become a society of dreamers, sitting back in idle contemplation of the Divine, giving only secondary importance to how this vision could be brought to expression in the mundane world. On the other hand Western society became infatuated with the world of Matter, stressing pragmatic utilitarian and hedonistic values without giving much thought to the inner light, the unmoved mover, or the eternal values which could be used as beacons illuminating an ultimate meaning behind our frenetic search for pleasure, fame, and security amidst the perishable world of the senses.

Perhaps what we are witnessing in the world today and each in our own way participating in is the development of a vision of a balance between these two extremes. The spirit provides a heart for materialism, and the material world puts flesh on the bones of spirituality. Being raised in the West and exposed to the East can produce just such an integrated vision that leads to a creative and satisfying posture toward life regardless of the "hand" one may be dealt.

Both sensuality and spirituality have a role to play in the cultivation of inner personal happiness and interpersonal harmony, which can be said to be the goals of life stated in most general terms. Exposure to both the sacred and mundane aspects of an "exotic" culture such as India cannot but contribute to our individual and collective search for enjoyment, understanding and fulfillment.

3

Three Steps

My consistent experience with traveling is that the first step of each journey is a step "away from." Last night, as I climbed aboard the bus that would take me to the San Francisco airport, I was vividly conscious of what I was leaving behind. For me this included dear friends, a comfortable and familiar community, the soothing rolling hills of west Marin County, a job, the security and ease of a home, the reassurance of the daily Chronicle newspaper, local entertainment opportunities, and my wardrobe and other possessions.

As I closed my eyes and took an emotional inventory, it was more difficult to discern what I was leaving behind and what I was carrying with me as baggage. The first thing I noticed was the now familiar ache in my heart resulting from my recent separation from my mate, Carolyn, and my two teenage stepchildren, Rachel and Aaron. We had lived together as a family for eight years until a couple of months ago when Carolyn decided she wanted/needed to live alone with the kids. My commitment to the relationship had been such that I always thought that no matter what I would do in life, it would always remain within the context of our "marriage," however that would be mutually defined and redefined. Now suddenly I am faced with the opposite scenario in which what was certain is now improbable and from the impossible must arise the likely. Beneath the revolutionary uncertainty simmer mixed emotions of rejection and liberation, failure and hope, anger and abiding good-will.

Nor has the dissolution of my marriage been the only loss and disruption in my life this year. At the end of last year I lost a promising year-long consulting contract with the Oakland Public School District when a six million dollar bookkeeping error was discovered in their budget figures. In April I developed a ruptured disc which presses on my sciatic nerve and makes sitting extremely painful. In May my father passed away. In the wake of all this, I felt the need to call "time out" for healing and reorientation.

For the adept traveler the second step, the one after the step "away from," becomes a step "toward," in which the pull of the future becomes equal to or greater than the drag of the past. This need not be a callous dissociation from dear ones and familiar environs, but often consists of a two-fold recognition that 1) affirms the inner presence of those apparently left behind and 2) realizes that the first step away from a friend is also the first step in the circuit which eventually leads one back again to that friend. In celebration of this paradox, the South Indians have a declaration of leave-taking, the "good-bye" of which translates literally as, "Let me go, so I may come."

Physical pain has the effect of narrowing one's self-consciousness to the affected areas of one's body, and emotional pain has the effect of narrowing one's overall self-identity to the affected social ego. However, I have learned through fifteen years (including three years living in India) of study and practice of Eastern spiritual disciplines such as Zen, Yoga, Vedanta, and Taoism, that contraction of one's identity can never lead to spiritual well-being. On the contrary, spiritual well-being is precisely the enlargement of self-identity beyond the confines of one's body and ego.

It seems natural then that with bruised self-esteem, sorely contracted self-identity and uncertain future, I would gravitate back towards India for healing, rejuvenation and reorientation. For many Westerners the Asian experience has the impact of being at once a soothing balm and an energizing spark for lives that have become cramped and weary with pressure, stress, routine or self-doubt.

In my six previous trips to India, I have become very familiar with and at home in the Indian culture, world-view and life-style, each of which is dramatically different from what exists in the United States. This time I look forward to the possibility of checking in on old friends and familiar haunts as well as exploring new territory and meeting previously unknown people.

The cornerstone of my journey will be an extended visit in India with my spiritual teacher, advisor, and friend for these past fifteen years—about whom there will be more later. At the same time I would be dishonest if I did not admit that I am also looking forward to the extravagant feast of sensuous impressions that dazzle the visitor to Asia. I am eager to absorb (and describe) the exotic spectacle of sights and sounds, fragrances, flavors, textures, and activities of day to day life in Asia. Yet unlike their Western counterparts, Asians treat the sensory aspects of life as symbolic of a deeper and more primary level of life's undercurrent. Traditionally for an Asian, the surface experiences of life both proceed from and lead one back to a hidden sustaining reality.

After an extended visit to Asia, I dare say one can never look at the sometimes thrilling and sometimes horrifying data of the senses in quite the same light again. Thus on this journey of retreat and regeneration I will be on the lookout for both the sights and insights of the places and people I encounter along the way.

For the master traveler, a role for which I claim only to be an aspirant, the third step is neither "away from" nor "toward" but simply "on the path itself" or "in the moment itself." From this point onwards, each new encounter becomes at once the goal and the way.

Thus it was most welcome when my reminiscences and reveries of past and future were interrupted by a fellow bus-passenger who began chatting with me about many things from jobs and man-woman relationships to sports and vacations. There was something charming and disarming about this young man's sincere and unassuming candor. I thought to myself, "As much as I love the friendly and welcoming manner of the people of India, it's great to be reminded on this very first leg of my trip that I need not travel 10,000 miles to enjoy this most basic of human characteristics." He seemed almost awed by the extent or scope of my trip (he was flying to San Diego) and seemed touched when I said I would recall with gratitude the gift of warmth and affinity with which he had christened my journey.

It's lucky I enjoy airports, because in the coming months I'm likely to see several of them. In spite of their aesthetic bankruptcy and ecological toxicity, airports remain for me exciting and fascinating places. They symbolize the uncanny mobility of modern society, which in ages gone by could only be approached or surpassed by the fanciful flights and winged meditations of dreamers, poets, and mystics. It can be counted at once a loss and a gain that people have come to take for granted the prejudice that this present form of mobility and freedom is superior to the previous emphasis. Ultimately I suppose it comes to pretty much the same thing. The challenge of maintaining inner stillness and stability in the midst of outer movement is as great a theme of artistic and spiritual tradition as is the envisioning and creating of extensive movement, activity and change in the silent stillness and imperturbable peace of one's inmost self.

Airports are particularly favorable haunts for confirmed people watchers such as myself. What an incredible range of people, races, ages, faces, styles of dress, demeanors, languages, moods, relationships, ways of walking and countless other features! There is a great commotion in which each individual constitutes his or her own center. Each of us seems pretty firmly enthroned as the protagonist or central character in the ongoing melodrama (or not so mellow drama) we call life. Yet to varying degrees each of us remains open and sensitive to countless touching scenes around us in which we are at once a detached witness and yet somehow identified with those whom we are sensitive to. Remaining sensitive to and identifying with the unfolding dramas in the lives of others ironically strengthens our ability to remain something of a detached observer in the midst of our own and vice versa.

It is said that foreign travel "broadens the mind and loosens the bowels." In addition it can stimulate the senses, pacify the heart and enlighten the soul. Most of these outcomes were in my mind as I planned this present journey. As I felt the plane lift off from the runway at San Francisco International, I could already hear the distant yet advancing call of the tropics in which I was to be immersed for at least the next six months of my life.

4

Close Enough To Pretend

There is a Grateful Dead song entitled "Saint of Circumstance" with a lyric which goes, "Well, this must be heaven / Or close enough to pretend." That line keeps dancing across my mind as an apt caption for my present experience. Half-lying, propped up against a small brick barrier on the sand of Coconut Beach just outside of Waikiki Beach in Hawaii, feeling the sun on my bare skin, listening to the sweet warbles of tropical birds counterpointed by the gently lapping surf of jade waters reflecting swaying coconut palms, set against a blue sky dappled with clouds which periodically break the heat, and with faint Plumeria fragrances punctuating the salt freshness during breaks in the soft off-shore breeze, my sense of inner well-being and comfort is as full as this sentence is long.

My dear friend John, with whom I am staying my five days in Hawaii, dropped me here this morning on the way to his nearby landscaping job. "What's the other name for Coconut Beach?" he slyly asked his co-worker Jan as I was slipping out of the truck. "Nude Beach" was Jan's smiling reply. If that is true, the three women and one man with whom I am sharing this 200 yard stretch of paradise are not honoring its intent.

Drowsily, my mind fills with images of my first trip to India. Initially I had not felt at all drawn to India. The picture I had developed from numerous books, magazines, newspapers, films and television depictions of India was primarily of poverty, squalor, and misery.

After graduating from Stanford University in 1969 and undergoing unsuccessful stints as a substitute teacher and as a graduate student in cinematography, I had retreated into the self-absorption of an identity crisis. Having assumed the identity of a student for seventeen of my twenty-two years of life, I was ill-prepared for choosing and devoting myself to some other productive and fulfilling role in society.

Selling my car and other possessions, I went with a friend to Europe for a change of scene and perspective. After a couple of months of touring, I took a summer job as a general laborer on a construction site in England and saved my shillings to return to the so-called "Hippie Caves" on the Greek Island of Crete. It was while living in the caves that I met numerous travelers either on their way to or returning from India, with tales of a friendly spiritual people, exotic scenes, tropical beaches and high times. Before the winter rains thinned out the population of New Age cave dwellers, I found myself part of the overland caravan through Turkey, Iran, Afghanistan, and Pakistan to India.

My initial impression of India did little to alter my preconceptions. Delhi and Bombay were over-crowded, squalid, and depressing. The only pleasant surprise of my first week in India had been that most everyone spoke some English. As a result of the school system having been inaugurated by the British during the colonial days, even now English is the medium for most of the educational system in India. As there are seventeen different indigenous languages being spoken on the Indian sub-continent, English has become the officially declared "link language" used between Indians from one part of the country and another. Whereas in Europe one can usually find someone who speaks "Tourist English," such as "The museum is over there" or "This hat costs five francs," in India one can even engage the locals in elaborate personal or philosophical discussions. This was to become a major endearing factor, which has called me back to India again and again.

On that first trip the scene changed dramatically the moment I disembarked from the ferry in Goa, a coastal state south of Bombay. With two other foreign travelers whom I had met on the ferry, I rented a cottage on Calangute Beach for less than a dollar a week. It was there that I concocted the scheme of learning Yoga while in India and returning to teach it in the U.S. Although predating the current craze for aerobic classes, there was just dawning an interest in suburban America for the physical and emotional benefits of Hatha Yoga. I figured to get in on the ground floor of what indeed was about to become a multi-million dollar industry. What neither the suburban housewives nor myself knew at the time was that the physical exercises comprise only a marginal component of the vast and profound system of yoga. I was soon to discover this.

I awake back on Coconut Beach with John crooning to me something about our being invited to visit some friends this afternoon out near Kaneohe Bay on the other side of the island. He tickles my fancy with visions of a stream in their back yard leading to a waterfall and swimming hole, with rocks for baking on and diving off. In all, this day makes me wonder if maybe the airplane that took off in San Francisco might not have just kept going up without coming down.

A modest come-down lurked around the corner.

5

Garbage in Paradise

Yes, even paradise has a dump! Most fittingly after reveling in the exquisite sensuousness of tropical luxuriance yesterday, I currently find myself in the cab of John's truck at the Kailua Dump. The windows are rolled up (itself an oddity in Hawaii) to keep out the stench and windblown particles of matter in various stages of decomposition. This is the end of the line for rubbish. If one had the stomach for it, one could discover more than anyone would want to know by rummaging through these forsaken traces of the waste of our throwaway materialistic culture.

When John slid out of the cab upon our arrival, he gathered up some miscellaneous trash that had accumulated inside — straws, plastic wrappers, paper cups and sacks, etc. Out of habit he looked around for a garbage can before realizing that we were parked inside one. With obvious pleasure he casually tossed the entire armful over his shoulder to flutter in the wind and fall where it may. He apparently found this action so liberating that he immediately stuck his head back in the cab and began searching hopefully for more trash. Litter therapy — but is it addicting?

This garbage in paradise reminds me that if I am not to romanticize India, I should be up front about some of its less appealing features. In order to enjoy and get the most out of India, I have found that there are a number of things that it is best to ignore. Examples of this are screechy music blaring from the scratchy speakers of churches, mosques, temples and tea-stalls at 5AM, the stink flowing in the gutter along the street just outside of most urban restaurants, the bare light bulb glaring all night six inches above your face while you try to sleep on a second class train berth, the tedium and ineptitudes of every bureaucratic venture from cashing traveler's checks to extending a visa, and the unsettling smile of "relief" on the face of the water buffalo soaking twenty feet upstream from where you are bathing. When asked about this last and perhaps most disconcerting situation on the above list, an Indian friend of mine replied with a shrug, "For thousands of years we have been living in close proximity with animals. It's nothing to us."

As far as I'm concerned, the jury is still out on whether the psychological peace gained through learning to ignore these factors is greater or less than the loss of physical hygiene and the damage to the nervous system that results from the Indian indifference to these and similar conditions. Of course, there are other problems which a Westerner definitely should not ignore, such as the fact that each glass of water is the habitat of a veritable ecosystem of microorganisms. The point I would like to make here is that there is a wealth of experience and insight to be gleaned from the India experience if we can resist the temptation to throw the baby out with the bath water, or in this case I suppose the temptation would be to throw the buffalo out with the river water.

My final couple of days in Hawaii (and the U.S.A.) were mostly spent running last minute errands: buying small gifts to take to people in India such as colored pencils, audio cassettes, lighters, pickled sushi ginger, miso, macadamia nuts and chocolate; processing and sending photos of a little friend's second birthday party celebrated the day I left San Francisco; completing my traveling stock of vitamins and herbs; taking care of eleventh hour business regarding insurance, finances, etc; purchasing a cap, chapstick, and sun protection cream; and paying daily visits to Chinatown for acupuncture treatments for my sciatica from Dr. Suen Hang

Yee, a genius at his art who charges a mere ten dollars per session.

Throughout the running around I would frequently be stilled by some physical reminder or another of the lush tropical setting which would otherwise recede behind the horizon of my consciousness. And as much as I would be taken by the particular feel of sun and breeze on my face or the glorious rainbow or haunting bird call, I would be even more struck with the role that *consciousness* itself plays in determining the quality of our experience. For example, we each take tens of thousands of breaths each day, and so long as they remain unconscious, they are "no big deal." But if in any given moment we pause and consciously observe and appreciate one single breath, we can hardly help but be filled with a sense of grace and wonder.

6

Three Strikes And You're In

The story of how I happened upon my teacher and met the many people in India with whom I have become very intimate over the past fifteen years is a convoluted one. One Sunday afternoon I was sitting at a beach front cafe in Calangute, sipping a *lassi* (yogurt drink) and chatting with an Indian tourist from Bombay who had come down to see the Western hippie settlement which had developed in Goa. After asking me if hippies worship the sun, because he had seen so many of them gazing silently at sunrises and sunsets, he asked me, "What is your mission in India?"

Although I had not really thought of this in terms of a mission, I responded, "I want to study Yoga."

"Well then, you surely must go down to Mahatma Gandhi College in Trivandrum. They have the most marvelous Yoga program there."

One week later I completed an exhausting three day overland journey to Trivandrum, the capital of Kerala State near the southernmost tip of India. In the midday tropical heat I lugged my backpack the last half mile up the tree-lined entrance road leading to the Mahatma Gandhi College gate. There was an eerie silence and haunting emptiness to the campus. The college was between sessions.

The gate was locked, and I had to create a minor ruckus to rouse anyone. Finally the caretaker appeared. He seemed peeved, but as he spoke no English, I could only surmise the exact cause. He eyed my backpack and motioned in universal sign language that I should go away. Just as I was about to turn and leave, I spotted a figure walking out of a building in the distance. I pointed him out to the caretaker who called the second man to come help.

When I explained to this one, who turned out to be a history teacher, how, why, and from where I had come, he had a good laugh. "I am so sorry, but the man who sent you here must not have been here for many years. We have not taught yoga here in the last decade."

Strike One!

When he saw how deflated I suddenly became, he told me of a yoga school a couple of miles walk through the jungle. After a nap and a shower on campus, I set out in search of the school. About an hour later I reached a compound with a large billboard out front announcing itself as a yoga school.

I presented myself as a potential applicant and was told that I would have to have an interview with the head guru first. I was ushered up to a second story office wherein lounged one of the most overweight men I had ever laid eyes on. "So you want to study yoga?" he asked. When I answered in the affirmative, he proceeded to ask me the following list of questions. Do you own a camera? Do you have a tape recorder? What does your father do? How much does he make?

Strike Two!

Now I felt totally misguided and adrift. I considered cutting the rest of my trip short and returning to San Francisco on the first available flight. It was in such a state of self-pity that I found myself in a restaurant that night. Even the appearance of a couple of hippies, the first I had seen since my setting off alone from Goa, didn't arouse me. Somberly I returned their greeting and continued sulking. Finally I was lifted out of my insularity into a state of kinship when I overheard them talking about the Grateful Dead. I joined their table and soon I was relating my predicament to them. One of them had heard of a good yoga school thirty miles north at a place called "Sivagiri Temple" in Varkala.

The next morning I caught a jammed bus to Varkala. Now I was truly off the beaten path, and my fellow passengers were enthusiastic in attempting to determine who I was and what they might be able to do for me. In Varkala I was let off and pointed toward a temple sitting atop one of the twin peaks jutting above a lush valley of rice paddy fields, coconut palms, mango, cashew, jackfruit, papaya, and banana trees.

Another bus stopped, and the driver asked, "Where going?" "Temple," was my reply. After some lively argument in the Malayalam language amongst the driver and passengers, they motioned me aboard. As we approached the temple without slowing down, I became agitated and made it clear that this is where I wanted to stop. As the temple receded behind us, agitation became aggravation. I felt as if I were being kidnapped. All the driver could or would say was, "O.K...O.K." He motioned for me to "cool it" as he sped up another hill and around another bend.

Approximately two miles past the temple, the bus halted across from the gate of a large compound. "Happy you here," said the bus driver, motioning for me to get off.

Strike Three!

In my anger, weariness, and loneliness at that time, little did I suspect that I was standing before a place that over the coming fifteen years was to become as familiar and dear to me as home. Looking back across those years, I can only marvel and wonder at the critical role played in my life by that Indian tourist from Bombay, the hippie in Trivandrum, and that bus driver in Varkala, each of whom became my greatest benefactors through their "errors" and "mistakes," without which I would never have been graced with the incredibly rich experiences and transformational insights which were to follow.

7

Time Flies (Coach Class)

It is hard to take "time" seriously when it can be monkeyed with so perplexingly. The calendar and the watch lord over modern society, demanding absolute allegiance. But now and then a peephole is glimpsed through the veil, no less dis-illusioning than the unmasking of the puny little man masquerading as the Wizard of Oz at the climax of that fable.

Six hours ago (or so it seems) it was 3:30AM on November 21. Now I am to believe it is 4:30AM November 22. That means the whole of November 21 squeezed into five hours. Am I a day older even if not a day wiser? One could age very rapidly by continuously flying westward around the globe.

This also calls to mind the recent decision by the United States congress to extend Daylight Savings Time by moving all clocks forward one hour, three weeks earlier than the traditional manipulation in late April. What precipitated this latest monkey-business? Some scientific discovery regarding the rate of rotation of the earth perhaps? Quite not. The successful lobbying effort, fueled by hundreds of thousands of dollars, was spear-headed by the charcoal briquette industry, whose marketing researchers estimated a windfall of several millions of dollars per year in extra sales of charcoal given one additional hour of daylight per evening for back yard barbecues during the first three weeks of April.

This new legislation was passed over the objections of

public health and safety exponents who pointed out that the increase in evening light for barbecues could only be acquired at the price of decreasing the early morning light when school children are on the roads and vulnerable to increased traffic accidents. Presumably if the flashlight industry had gotten its act together, we might have done away with daylight savings time all together.

Time, it now appears, is more a collective agreement than a thing in and of itself. As I once heard a Zen teacher remark during a lecture, "If three or more people get together and decide to call a rock 'a turtle,' it is a turtle."

Time also flies backwards. The eleven hour flight from Honolulu to Hong Kong provides a great deal of time for mental "home movies," and I have enjoyed my share on this flight. Naturally some of them picked up the thread of my initial visit to India:

The bus, having dumped me out in the middle of somewhere that I mistook for "nowhere," disappeared in its own dust. I made my way in a daze to the gateway across the road. Although Providence was leading me by the hand, I was convinced that I was lost. Only since then have I come to realize that a sign which reads "GODISNOWHERE" can signify the imminent presence of the Divine (God is now here) just as well as it can suggest the non-existence of the Divine (God is nowhere). The difference is in the mind of the interpreter.

Upon reaching the gate I see an Indian man with curly gray hair and a long white beard. The scene is washed with tranquillity, but I have far from internalized it. The bearded man, dressed in a light orange sheet, looks up and laughs. Suddenly I too see the image his retina is receiving (me!), and I join in his laughter, releasing some of my tension. He doesn't speak English, but he sends a couple of beautifully smiling boys to get someone who does.

Soon a handsome young man smiles up to me, takes one of my hands in his and welcomes me. He waits without releasing my hand. The tension in the muscles of my body eases away. He releases my hand. I tell him what I am looking for. He informs me that this is a *gurukula*, a combination home, school, and temple. They do not teach physical yoga exercises as such, but they do teach and practice yoga in its broadest sense. He remarks that I appear weary and invites me to stay and rest up.

I am led part way down a hillside to a small one room cottage overlooking a grove of coconut palms shading the peaceful yet active Indian village below. Singing, chanting, drumming and laughter float up to the porch. I utter the international tourist refrain, "How much for the room?" And I am told, "You need not pay anything. It is here for you."

In addition I am informed as to what time the communal meals are served up at the Gurukula and invited to also join in on the morning and evening sessions for prayer, meditation, and chanting. No pressure is put on me to participate. For the two weeks of my residency I am never asked to help prepare the meals, nor clean up after them, nor to contribute financially. It is evident that their only concern regarding me is my own happiness. Naturally, after a couple of days, this treatment makes me all the more eager to contribute and participate as well as to learn from them.

I learn that the function of a gurukula is to provide at least a temporary refuge for people who want to remove themselves from the workaday worries and pressures of economic, social, and habitual patterns of life, to contact the essential in themselves and to take a quiet look at who they are deep down and what they wish to become. It is described as stepping out of the current of one's life and sitting comfortably on the bank for a time, observing the river flow without being carried away by the drift.

One fascinating feature of the gurukulas is that, for the most part, it has been found unnecessary to define or assign duties, yet what needs to be done always gets accomplished with relatively few conflicts in the process. When spiritual values are given primacy in a group, through the inner consent of each individual, then there arises a harmony regarding the secondary although necessary aspects of life.

In such a setting, action itself becomes a mere reflection or expression of the light or spirit that is savored during one's more receptive or contemplative moments. Nature's ceaseless but silent work of bearing forth, nourishing and sustaining becomes the model of action for the contemplative. When one's unclouded vision reveals that something needs to be done, one simply uses one's body as an instrument to accomplish the deed without allowing the mind or spirit to become ensnared in the meshes of hope, fear, or other extraneous factors that normally accompany action. At least that is the ideal, and it seems to operate fairly well in actuality.

There were eight or ten elementary school aged boys boarding at this gurukula, receiving tutoring from the older inmates and also receiving twice daily lessons in the spiritual traditions of India. Each evening after the songs, meditation and lesson, the boys were given an opportunity to air any gripes, complaints or accusations from their day's interactions. With Prasad, the bright young manager of the gurukula, presiding there would ensue a lively discussion including the defense of the accused party. The beauty was that Prasad somehow or another always seemed to defuse the tension. By humor and bringing in a wider perspective, he took the edge off of what previously appeared as earth-shaking to one party or another. At the same time he did not overlook the inconsiderations that one boy may have shown to another.

The discussions were carried on in Malayalam, so most of this I had to intuit and infer from tones, facial expressions, and other emotional indications. When punishments were deemed necessary they usually consisted of chewing bitter leaves, but occasionally a large shaven twig, the size which goes "whoooooosssh" when waved through the air, was employed to strike the hand of the guilty party.

This initially disturbed me greatly as for some time I had felt absolutely opposed to physically violent punishment. Upon reflection it became evident to me that Nature itself has violent methods of correcting imbalances and overcoming disturbing tensions. Vomiting is one example of a natural process which can be understood in this light. Still something about corporeal punishment didn't sit right with me.

On one evening Ganga, Prasad's chief assistant and a teacher at the school across the road, deemed it necessary to inflict such a punishment. As I watched I could easily see that the two sharp blows with the twig gave more pain to Ganga than to the child.

The child cried, but five minutes later could be seen playing and laughing. An hour later I met Ganga who was still downcast. He said that he went through some "soul searching" whenever he was forced into a position of judicial authority. To him, though, the main thing was to feel love rather than anger. He said he would never strike or punish a student if he found that he himself was acting out of the emotional imbalance which inevitably accompanies anger. In such a case, he would let someone else take over rather than bruise a student with his anger, which he felt stings much deeper and can disable for much longer than surface pain. That seemed to me like a very enlightened and seldom observed constraint upon "spanking" whether in the home or in the classroom.

During that first exposure to the Narayana Gurukula, the guru himself was out of town having an eye operation. Nearly twenty of his Western students were two hundred miles north building and planting on the island property which had been recently donated to him for the establishment of another gurukula.

Looking back, I feel it was fortunate for me to land at the gurukula when the guru was out. If my first impression of the gurukula had been of a place where philosophy was 'taught," I probably would have left after a couple of days. In all my years of previous schooling, I had come to regard philosophy as a dry intellectual exercise removed from the heart and soul of life. But as it was, I was afforded the opportunity to sample the fruit of the philosophy firsthand which then whet my appetite to know what view of the world allowed my hosts to be so gracious, generous, undemanding, bright, vibrant, and at peace with themselves and each other. If a philosophy could lead to such celebrative peace and serene vibrancy in both individual and collective life, then I was darn well going to investigate it.

8

The Indian Honeymooners

My aisle-mates on this leg of the journey (Honolulu – Hong Kong) are a handsome young Indian couple – she of fine delicate features, long eyebrows and large deep brown eyes and he of short black hair, pleasantly pudgy cheeks, polyester clothes and an over-sized silver watch. I find myself wondering if they married for love or parents. In a way that I recognize as typically Indian, they are very tender with one another, even discretely caressing each other in the covert manner characteristic of the new generation of Indians. Fifteen years ago, on-screen kissing was not permitted in Indian movies.

As they seem very wrapped up in one another, and I am feeling somewhat shy (I must not have my travel legs beneath me yet), our communication does not exceed a few friendly nods. And yet just as the Marin Airporter bus passenger sent me off from my home-base, I feel as if in some way this couple is silently welcoming me back into the world of India.

...No sooner did I close the journal after the last sentence, than did the young man, as if on cue, lean over towards me and smile. He paused, and I reciprocated to his subtle opening with a question about their destination. They are on a "round the world" honeymoon. He is a pharmacist in Wales, and neither of them has been back to India in ten years. When he sat back, she leaned forward and began interviewing me, which was a rare treat for me, as non-westernized Indian women are far more reserved.

It tickled me that they had been unsuspecting victims of the geographical rivalry between Los Angeles and San Francisco. They had planned to spend four days in each city, but their host in L.A. had assured them there was nothing to see in or around San Francisco that they couldn't see in one day. They extended their L.A. stay accordingly and then felt terribly short-changed in S.F. This can serve as a good warning to me on this trip to not necessarily accept as gospel the biases and prejudices of the people whom I meet and upon whom I will be depending, to some extent, to guide my movements.

I recall my first hosts in India. I was riding a bus down the west coast from Goa to Kerala. When my seat-mate learned I was from the U.S.A., he started asking me questions about the World Heavyweight Boxing Champion, Cassius Clay. I described to him the so-called "Ali Shuffle." He invited me to spend the night with his family and then continue my journey refreshed in the morning.

His name was Anthony Roche. He was a Roman Catholic with five sisters, three brothers, a pregnant wife, and a father-in-law who thinks population is the number one problem in the world today. If not in the world, then at least population was the problem in the very small house in which the entire above-mentioned family resided. Indians do not have the same requirements for privacy which we in the West have. Whereas each of us wants our own bedroom, they would find such an arrangement drab and "lonely." It is interesting that Indians tend to be communal socially and individualistic spiritually, whereas we tend to be individualistic socially and communal spiritually.

The Roches took me in and treated me like a brother, feeding me a sumptuous meal of rice and curries, offering me beer, and trying to hide their disappointment in finding out that I was less than mediocre on the guitar I was carrying. I slept under the security of a mosquito net and upon waking in the morning was immediately notified that water had been heated for my bath (my first hot water in over a month). After my bath I returned to my room to find two fried eggs, a cup of coffee, fresh chipatis (flat bread), and a liter of boiled water for my canteen.

I felt like I had fallen into a Hobbit novel. I have found that throughout the world people are generally loving toward their family and friends, but what often sets one culture apart from another is the way in which strangers are viewed and treated.

As I've traveled the past fifteen years, I've also become aware of some law of inverse relation between generosity and affluence. Perhaps it's true that the more you have, the more you feel you have to lose. Of course, this law allows for many exceptions, but for the most part it seems to hold true. In India people will lavish what they have on a stranger even if it means depriving themselves. In the West often people with more than they can use plus thousands of dollars in reserve will still begrudge a stranger or even an acquaintance some food, shelter and/or a ride somewhere.

One major exception to this law of inverse ratio between affluence and generosity was awaiting me in Singapore where I had a three day layover before the flight which would land me back in India.

9

Singapore's Veneer

Singapore is a fascinating, if not altogether enchanting, place. Three ethnic currents flow parallel to constitute its cultural identity: Chinese, Malay and Indian. The common thread and meeting ground is an unabashed mercantilism that has assumed the proportions of a national creed. A guide book I read on the plane from Hong Kong opened with the ironically boastful claim that visitors to Singapore expecting traces of pre-modern quaintness and quieter times will be surprised at the commercial dynamism that thrives as the nation's life-blood.

To me that seems like a back-handed endorsement, but within the frame of reference of the shared values of Singaporeans, it bespeaks the fulfillment of a collective aspiration. Of course, each geographical region is going to have its own particular value-system. Herb Caen, the San Francisco columnist, once wrote (in the early 1970's) that the two most common questions asked of a new acquaintance in New York were "What's your salary?" and "How much rent do you pay?" whereas in San Francisco they were, "What's your sign?" and "Who's your guru?"

This morning I was inside an "Art Centre" gift shop, and my eye was caught by a glossy book entitled *Colourful Scenery of Singapore*. I thumbed through it, and fully one half of the photographs were of the concrete jungle glowingly captioned in the book as "Singapore's Commercial Centre."

Colorful scenery indeed! I guess aesthetics are a matter of taste.

This cultural and aesthetic relativism would be further demonstrated three months later when I passed through Singapore on my way back from India. Coming from the U.S., I found Singapore something of an embarrassment (seeing the extremes to which commercialism could go). Coming from India, I would find Singapore simply a marvel. After three months of not seeing a building over three stories, a road wider than barely two lanes, or a single department store, Singapore with its forest of skyscrapers, ribbons of divided highways and clumps of chrome and glass shopping malls would take my mind and senses by storm.

Still there are four very positive things about Singapore which have made my experience here more than simply a layover in transit. The first is the tropical climate with its unencumbering side-effects of being heatingless, blanketless, sockless and often sleeveless. Secondly, I thoroughly enjoyed the traditional "Hawker Centres" consisting of foodstalls of delicious Chinese, Malay and Indian dishes, such as "Vegetable Bee Hoon" (noodles, tofu, vegetables, quail eggs, and gravy). Thirdly, I can whole-heartedly recommend the Corralarium on Sentosa Island, with living exhibits of tropical corral in heart-stoppingly beautiful colors and forms. Finally, I must honor the loving and generous Kashyap family in whose palatial home I have stayed. The Kashyaps are an Indian family that is fully westernized except for the Eastern spirituality and hospitality of the elders and the patience and sweet sensitivity of the four kids aged nine to twenty two. May their tribe increase.

I originally got to know the Kashyaps as students and devotees of my Indian teacher. Three years ago during one of my previous stays in India, the two teenage Kashyap daughters, Kiran & Savita, joined the Guru in his gurukula mountain retreat where I was also studying. In practice a gurukula combines in a single setting the aspects of home, school, and temple. Thus living, learning, and worshiping are brought into intimate connection.

Kiran and Savita raised many eyebrows among the local population because of their westernized teen manner coupled with their Indian ancestral appearance. I remember one night in particular when an American friend and I extended the situation to its logical absurdity by covering the bare light bulbs in the prayer hall with red paper and dancing with Kiran and Savita to the rock beat of the cassette tapes they had brought with them (*Gurukula a Go Go*). The girls invited me to stay at their house on my way through Singapore when returning to the U.S. a month later, and I have been made to feel as a part of their extended family ever since.

Sashilal, the father, is a very successful businessman who has made his fortune importing and exporting carpets. Urmalji, in addition to being a dedicated mother of four, is very active in community volunteer work and practices sitar daily. The family is very nicely rounded out by a very serious-minded eldest son and an extremely impish youngest daughter.

It is one of the inspiring and reassuring benefits of travel that one is invited to touch and be touched by families such as this one far from the protective yet often confining environs of one's own immediate family. My past experiences bolster me with the confidence that several more such families await me around as yet unimagined corners on this present journey.

10

A Passing Shadow

Strange occurrences on the way to take-off tonight. First off, when the Madras bound plane was full and we were all buckled in, they announced a delay. It seems one of the passengers on our flight was traveling with a forged passport. Airport regulations require that the three pieces of that fellow's luggage, which earlier had been checked-in, also be removed from the plane for fear they may contain a bomb or other contraband. The only way that could be accomplished was by pulling off all the luggage until the pieces in question were found.

One hour later all was settled. As we were "pushing back" from the loading ramp and listening to the last minute safety instructions, there was a commotion a few rows up and across the aisle from me. Apparently someone had passed out. The plane pulled back to the ramp, and after thirty minutes the man was pronounced dead. Next it was announced that before we could leave, the police were going to need to come aboard and conduct a brief investigation which would take up to another hour.

The upshot of all this was that we took off at 12:30AM on the 26th rather than 9:00PM on the 25th, and we were minus two passengers. It was hard to feel very grumpy about it. Each of us who remained had felt the shadow of death sweep ever so close, while sparing us for at least one more night.

Nothing distinguishes Eastern thought from Western so

much as the respective viewpoints on death. It seems most natural to us in the West to view death as an ending, but in Indian thought death instead marks the beginning of each new cycle. A fruit must sever connection with its source of life, the tree, fall to the ground and decay in order that the seed of the new tree can take root and grow. The sea's water is dissolved into thin air where it forms pregnant clouds. The cloud's moisture is dispersed so that all below may live and be nourished. The moon wanes to total emptiness before it begins to wax toward a new fullness. In respiration, an expiration must precede each inspiration.

In Hindu theology Siva is presented as the God of Death and Dissolution. Were it not for his ruthless smashing of the morbid husk which tends to become encrusted around any creation, be it in the world of physical bodies, emotional fixations, mental concepts or even psychic and spiritual expressions, then there could be no new creation. The chicken would remain in the shell, the fetus in the womb, the sprout within the seed, and the future would suffocate within the "cosmic egg."

Although such a viewpoint may seem foreign to us, it is far from a purely intellectual exercise. Earlier this year my father passed away. Naturally my first reaction was of loss and sorrow, which I shared with my mother and two brothers. But an interesting turn came when my brothers and I discussed the plans for his memorial service. First of all, we decided to mix his ashes with the soil at the foot of a freshly planted star magnolia tree, not only as a memorial, but also as living testimony to the continuation of the life which had been our father.

At the small memorial service we held with a number of my father's closest friends, we all spoke of what my father had meant to each of us. As we went around the circle, it became inspiringly clear that we were not simply speaking in the past tense, but were speaking of a dynamic presence with its own special texture. We knew my father's presence would continue to exert an impact on our lives with the persistent stamp of his unique spirit.

Tonight as the passing shadow of death whispers again to me my father's name, sense of loss is counter-balanced by a sense of gain, and the sense of an ending is nearly obliterated by a satisfying sense of continuity and fresh beginnings in which my father remains an intimate and influential participant. This morning when I land in Madras, I will be seeing India for and through both of us.

11

Benign Chaos

My fourth floor balcony overlooks the Egmore Railway Station in Madras. The word "hubbub" doesn't quite do justice to the scene below, even with "hellava" added as a prefix. There is a great clamor of noise and movement, and yet strangely there is something mellow or peaceful about it. This must be because the hubbub does not consist of numerous conflicting or competing individual elements but is rather symphonic or holistic in its seeming chaos.

The entire scene is presided over by the two-square-block structure which is Egmore Station itself. The station building is a grand combination of colonial victorian and Moslem mosque. The fact that such a seemingly incongruous blend "makes it" architecturally is an illustration of what I am trying to describe as peaceful chaos.

Two-tone green open-air buses, yellow bug-like three wheeler "auto-rickshaws" (the golf carts that move a nation), multicolored bicycle-rickshaws, taxis, fancifully painted trucks, motorcycles, bicycles, street cart vendors, cows, dogs, and pedestrians, all weave in and out of each other in a pattern suggestive of the web of a spider on L.S.D. And yet no harsh words are exchanged, and even the horns, bells and buzzers seem more like simple self-declarations than threats. Boys pass by in shorts, women in saris, and girls and men in skirts.

Some images from my 3:30AM bus ride from the Madras

airport into town: a waning half-moon that seemed to be almost dripping with enchantment, perhaps from all the dreams of those sleeping here below; white-sheet shrouded bodies curled up in doorways and beneath bus shelters who, given that I had been forced to sit up all night, elicited rather more envy than pity; fluorescent-lit tea stalls with small nocturnal gangs of men circling around shopkeepers mixing tea, milk and sugar by pouring it back and forth at arm's length from dipper to dipper; small groups of early-bird women with saris pulled up between their legs, beating the morning rush to the district water-tap, cleaning last night's pots and pans, filling jugs, washing clothes and gossiping, much as their ancestors have done for centuries, with the main difference being that the village well has been replaced by a spigot; young men hosing down lorries with the dim light only hinting at the wildly colorful hand-painted scenes covering their four sides; and billboard after billboard beckoning those below to forsake their simple roots and join the consumer society through possession of this or that modern "convenience."

The bus let me down at the Taj Coromandel Hotel in Madras where my friend, Mr N.C. Kumaran, was to be waiting to drive me back to his home. Given the lateness of my flight and the hour, I was not surprised that Kumaran was not there. But I was surprised to learn, upon calling his house, that he and his wife were staying in the hospital as he was recovering from some unexpected surgery. Thus I found myself stranded at 4AM, on less than two hours sleep, without knowing where to throw my pack or lay my head.

12

A City Awakens

The Taj, where I stood, is a luxury hotel with the cheapest room renting for 720 rupees—about 600 rupees above my "splurge rate." The night manager was very kind. When I had asked for a pay phone to call the Kumarans, he had given me free use of the hotel phone. When he learned of my predicament, he called a less expensive hotel nearby. They were fully booked. I decided to go find a hotel myself near Egmore Station, which was centrally located. From there it would be easy for me to go to a bank to change money, the airlines office to reconfirm my flight to Cochin, a bookstore to get postcards, the post office to send a telegram to Guru in Cochin, and the hospital to visit the Kumarans.

The manager called an auto-rickshaw, the driver of which upon seeing the paleness of my skin, insisted on charging over four times the normal fare. The manager entered the argument on my behalf and upon failing to budge the driver, offered to send me in the hotel car. "Just tip the driver (of the hotel car) whatever you wish." All of this free aid and support would be unlikely even for a guest at a swank Western hotel and nearly unthinkable for a non-guest.

A pre-dawn stillness, like the calm before a storm, surrounded Egmore Station as I drove up with my personal chauffeur. There's something I love very much about Indian cities in the very early morning. The air is cool and fresh, which in the heat and stench of the evening before would have seemed a remote improbability. There's a calm quiet which actually exerts a positive thrust, again owing to its contrast with the hectic clamor of the day before and the day to come. Everybody on the street is newly bathed and groomed, and even clothes are free of wrinkles and grime.

This is the time of day, between soft night dreams and harsh midday demands, that the four thousand year old spiritual and contemplative heritage of ancient India seems to exert its waning influence on its present day inhabitants. Most Indians still observe some brief prayer or ritual in the early morning, and it's almost as if for a few moments at this time each day there is actually a hint of uncertainty as to the outcome of the clashing culture, life style and values of the simple forms, patterns and profound religiousness of the past on the one hand and the crass commercial consumerism of the modern era on the other hand.

As I strolled from the car to the lodge, I noticed that already the traffic was beginning to pick up and that neither the pace nor the expressions of the passersby were as unhurried or as unharried as when I had begun these reflections just moments before.

The first lodge we tried, The Madras Tourist Home, was also "full-up," but they directed us a block away to Chandra Internationale Lodge where for fifty-five rupees ($4.50) I booked a room with a cement floor, wooden cot with foam mattress, one straight back chair, an Indian style bathroom with squatting toilet, a clothesline, and an overhead fan. This wasn't the Taj, but on the other hand neither was it the first hotel room I had occupied in South India fifteen years ago and which had prompted me to write in my journal:

> As a teenager I once went to a burlesque show on South State Street in Chicago. After the show, curiosity led me upstairs to the "flop house" where the "bums" were living. I think the same architect designed this hotel. Anyway there's these same walls which only reach halfway to the ceiling, leaving all the inhabitants as hopelessly together as they are hopelessly separated.

Noting with relief the cleanliness of the room, I switched on the fan, turned off the light and lay down on the bed. As it was just turning 6:00, I figured I could catch at least two or three hours of sleep before getting up for the day. This turned out to be impossible given the external excitement of a city awakening and the internal excitement of being back in India.

13

Reinitiations

At 6:30 I got up, washed my clothes by hand and took my first of what I knew would be many cold water bucket-and-dipper baths. Feeling surprisingly refreshed, I packed up the Japanese pickled ginger and American chocolates I had brought for Mrs. Kumaran and walked down to the bus stop to ride to Vijaya Hospital. When I first sat down on the 3/4 full bus, I assumed the intensified chattering and tittering was the common reaction to the presence of a funny looking Westerner (all Westerners are funny looking), but then I realized I had plopped down right in the middle of the "women only" section. In a feeble face-saving effort I remained seated in as dignified and circumspect a posture as possible. At the first stop I got up, by which time the "men's section" was full, and I had to stand in the aisle for the forty minute journey.

Even though it was not yet visiting hours, I was ushered to the hospital room like a proper "sahib." The Kumarans were surprised and happy to see me. They had not received the letter announcing the details of my arrival.

I had originally stayed with the Kumarans in their Madras home ten years ago with my teacher. Since then I have stayed with them several times and then had the rare pleasure of being able to host them during a California visit. Mr. Kumaran is a well-to-do retiree with a childlike sense of humor and wonder. He loves to discuss philosophical or spiritual matters. His round face, broad grin and big spectacles give him the appearance of a cuddly version of the old cartoon character Mr. Magoo. His wife is a soft-spoken small woman who lives and breathes (rather than talks) spirituality.

I hope it is not condescending to say that these are simple innocent people. It would be so only if I myself placed a high value on sophistication. But I am very much in sympathy with the dictionary definitions of sophisticate: "To alter deceptively; adulterate; to deprive of genuineness, naturalness or simplicity" and sophistication: "The process or result of making impure or weak; adulteration." It is at once comic and tragic that modern Western society has come to place sophistication as one of its cultural ideals and achievements and to look at it as even necessarily desirable. In any case, South Indians, in general, and the Kumarans in particular, don't have it.

They were just sitting down to breakfast, and Mrs. Kumaran insisted I join her husband by eating her share. From years of exposure to Indian hospitality, I knew it was useless to resist, though my protestations would be appreciated. Protestation, in this case, substitutes for a more overt display of gratitude which sometimes even shocks and offends the Indian sensibility.

During my first couple of visits to India this was an aspect of the culture that baffled me. I noticed when people did things for one another, there was no overt expression of gratitude, such as our convention of saying "Thank you." I found it slightly unnerving at first not to have my actions acknowledged by a show of gratitude. What struck me as even more strange was that when I would thank someone for a kind gesture, they would seem perplexed and even a bit put off.

Finally I asked my teacher about this, and he explained: "Suppose you get a cut on your left hand. With your right hand you will clean and bandage the wound. When you have finished, your left hand will not display any gratitude by stroking and caressing the right hand. It is simply taken for granted that as the two hands belong to the same self, they will naturally work together.

"A person raised in India may help a stranger with the same sense of self-identity as the right hand helps the left. To them, all are extensions of a single Self and will naturally attend to each other like two limbs of a single organism. People in India are not afflicted with the strong ego-sense of separate individuality that is conditioned in the West. Thus when you do say, 'Thank You,' people are put off by the implication of separateness and the suggestion that perhaps you expected less of them."

I have found that it is not that an Indian does not feel gratitude, but rather that all gratitude is directed to the one Self of all or to "God," as some refer to that all-pervasive Self of which we are each a part. Surely a book could be written exploring such subtleties of cross-cultural etiquette.

Thus my first Indian meal was destined to be a hospital serving of *idli* (steamed rice flour cakes) and vada (deep-fried gram flour doughnuts) with *sambar* (a thin curry stew) and coconut *chutney* (sauce). It tasted fairly good, although frankly I hardly noticed, so engrossed was I in a far-ranging conversation with the Kumarans that slipped easily between gossip, updates about mutual acquaintances, and relevant aspects of Guru's teachings as they applied to the unfolding life-dramas of each and all. After about an hour I excused myself to take care of my onward travel business with a promise to return again in the evening.

I enjoyed my day of moving about Madras, having something of a feeling of family and homecoming with the various officials, shopkeepers, bureaucrats and passersby with whom I interacted. Even the several beggars whom I encountered seemed to have been expecting me as I, indeed, had been them. All of this implied a unique blending of the personal with the impersonal which is characteristic of the Indian view of selfhood.

It was not always so, but strangely I have come to see it as a gift to me that I am given the opportunity to give to beggars. I welcome the opportunity to share my good fortune and, in a sense, feel as if I am in a small way repaying a debt I have to the Indian people for all that has been done for me.

In the West there is a stigma with being poor and worse is the shame heaped upon the head of one who stretches his or her hand. In India, beggars are treated neither as bad people nor nuisances.

Once in India while sitting with my teacher in a train compartment, stopped at a station, a dark arm pocked with scars reached through our window with palm upturned. "Isn't it beautiful," my teacher said as he transferred a portion of his lunch into the hands of the beggar boy. "Say what?" I thought, "Whatever else it might be, I wouldn't call it beautiful." "What?" is all I said aloud.

"This boy's trust in perfect strangers. He has that much faith in human kindness to reach out in need to us. Don't you see how in a way he is honoring us? Of course, there is much we might do to change society at large and with this boy in particular to help him become more self-reliant, but that should not obscure our appreciation of his immediate need." I have found that Indians tend to take the insightful sentiment, "There but for the Grace of God go I" one step further and actually think, "There go I."

Within all the hustle and bustle of my first day back in India, I detected a phenomena which became very familiar to me during my five years of traveling with my teacher and which I have recently lost touch with. It is the paradox of a very gentle and mellow pace and tempo experienced from within each moment at the same time that one activity follows immediately upon another without any lapse. Perhaps it is like residing in the eye of a hurricane which remains perfectly calm in itself though traveling hundreds of miles an hour.

Through my study of Eastern thought and my proximity and identity with my teacher, I discovered a still center at my own core which remains undisturbed by all the surface agitation and subterranean turmoil. If one makes one's home in that "space of the heart," one can be at home in the most foreign or unfamiliar settings. In fact, all spiritual disciplines have as their ultimate intention the establishing of one's self in this so-called "Center in the Midst of Conditions" or "Kingdom of Heaven Within" which is referred to variously as "The Absolute," "The True Self," or—as it is identical with the Self of all—"God."

Next to no attention is given in the mainstream of American culture and education to the cultivation of this profound and lofty constant at the core of one's own being. Hence there are many misconceptions about it, the most glaring of which perhaps is the belief that a life devoted to this kind of "self-realization" is necessarily a passive and antisocial one. The opposite is closer to the truth. Fearlessness is the natural by-product of identity with the eternal and imperturbable substratum of one's self and that of others. This wide identity motivates one to compassion toward all others (who are no longer seen as "other"). Self-realization, in this sense, frees one from the chronic insecurity which stems from seeing oneself as an ultimately separate being competing with the "other" in a struggle for survival. This dynamic is expressed poetically in a verse from the Indian scripture, *The Isavasya Upanishad*:

> To one who sees one's own self in all beings
> And all beings in one's own self,
> What craving, what delusion, what revulsion, what sorrow
> Can there be for one who sees only the oneness.

From a street-vendor I sipped my favorite drink in the world (or a close second to cool fresh water), tender coconut juice. I had a very good lunch of rice, six side curries, yogurt, soup and sweet pudding (seconds of everything included) for $.50, approximately double the price from my last visit three years ago. I slept a couple of hours under the ceiling fan in the afternoon, ventured out again by bus to buy stamps and send a telegram to Guru announcing my arrival tomorrow, returned to bathe and, refreshed once more, sat out on the balcony to observe and reflect upon the scene of tumultuous harmony below.

14

The Empty Boat

After a refreshing and inspiring two week stay at the gurukula during my first visit back in 1971, I had decided to continue on with my tour. First I planned to take a train to Rameswaram at the tip of India, and from there I would take the ferry to Ceylon (now Sri Lanka). At that point it was most likely that I would not have anything more to do with the gurukula.

So it might have been, had it not been for a fortuitous request made by the acting manager of the gurukula. He informed me of a World Parliament of Religions that was to be held in Kerala during the next month, and he asked me if I would be willing to deliver a paper on the *I Ching* (Book of Changes), the ancient Chinese wisdom oracle he had seen me studying. I accepted the invitation, and thus destiny was satisfied that I would be returning to the gurukula and meeting Nataraja Guru and his chief disciple Swami Nitya, who would also be attending the conference.

The word guru is most simply translated as "teacher," but the significance is more profound. Guru literally means "that which dispels darkness." The only thing which dispels darkness is light. When one combines this literal meaning with the fact that in India a guru is considered to be a "seer," one arrives at the image of a light which can see itself or of an all-witnessing eye which is at the same time the source of illumination. Thus the guru represents the eternal principles of enlightenment and insight.

In Indian philosophy darkness symbolizes ignorance, and light symbolizes knowledge. Ignorance is said to be the cause of bondage and suffering, whereas knowledge of the Real spells liberation and happiness. Just how this is so constitutes the story within a story of this present journal. At this early stage, suffice it to say that a guru functions as a mirror for a student's own inner resources of enlightenment.

Three weeks after leaving that first time, I was back at the gurukula. I arrived a couple of days before the return from the U.S.A. and Europe of Swami Nitya. Swami Nitya was at that time the chief disciple and designated successor of Nataraja Guru, the seventy-six year old founder and head of the Narayana Gurukula Movement. There was an electric air of anticipation about the gurukula as the children and adults alike prepared to give Swami Nitya a hero's welcome.

Thus I was surprised when I entered his room at 1:00AM, having asked to be awakened upon his arrival, to find a very unassuming and soft-spoken man working his way through a large pile of mail which had preceded him. Although most of the others were standing respectfully around the perimeter of the room, he motioned for me to take a seat and asked a few questions about who I was and whether I was feeling comfortable at the gurukula.

I once heard patience described as "the ability to stand still for another person." As Swami Nitya spoke with each person, I had the distinct feeling that he was fully present and that, for him, only that person mattered at that moment. He was able to pull this off in spite of the fact that he often had several ongoing conversations at once and a number of letters open before him. Yet each person and concern to which he turned his attention seemed to be bathed in a beacon of light.

The swami's long dark grey hair, long light grey beard and obviously well-pleased stomach gave him the appearance of an Indian Santa Claus. He spoke ever so softly as if apologizing for disturbing the natural silence. If one wished to hear him, one had to strain to hear, and yet the wisdom of his words was so enticing that when he spoke,

An inspirational facet of Indian life is the sacrelization of the mundane: Water, for example, is a divine gift from the heavens.

1-3. Much time is devoted to daily chores such as drawing water from village wells for cooking, drinking, and cleaning. Gratitude for nature's generosity transforms drudgery into a spiritually uplifting act.

4. People also travel thousands of miles to purify themselves in rivers such as the Ganges or under waterfalls such as this one in Tamilnad.

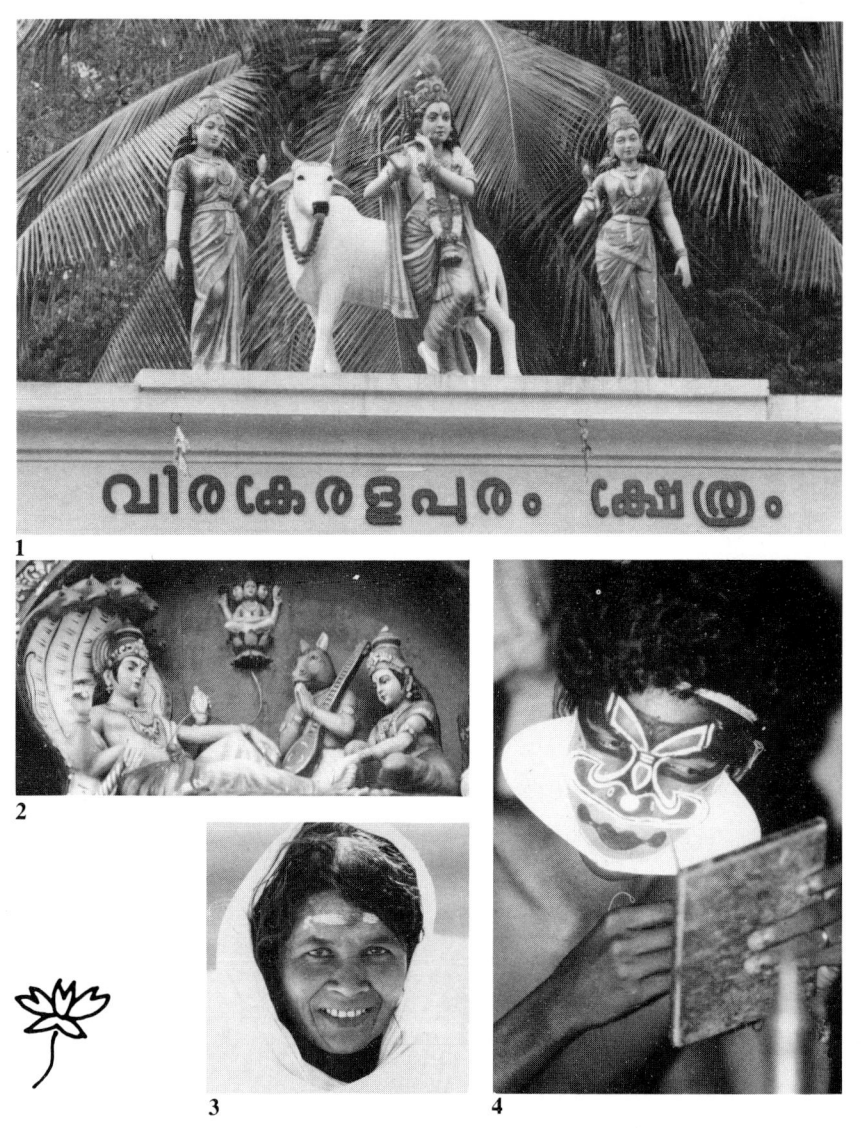

1-2. Rich religious imagery depicts the behavior and qualities of India's innumerable gods and goddesses. This symbolism inspires living and breathing expression in the chosen paths of many Indian people.

3. This woman is a *sannyasini*, a religious mendicant who has renounced home and possessions to live in the bounty of "God-consciousness."

4. Having spent years in disciplined practice of classical Hindu dance, this man spends another three hours applying the make-up for a twelve hour performance.

Utilitarian societies tend to see children as "not yet productive," and the elderly are often shunted aside as "no longer productive." In the Indian mind a special glow of grace surrounds the very young and the very old. If anything, the middle years of "responsibility" are tolerated as a dreamlike bridge between these two states of grace. Consequently a special quality of light and contentment can be seen on the faces of the young and the old, which a rare few never lose in between.

India provides a striking contrast to the West's technologically driven haste and waste. Whether eating rice and curries with one's fingers off of bio-disposable banana leaf plates, traveling from place to place to the clomp and rumble of bullock carts, or studying ancient scriptures, there is a simplicity and timelessness to Indian life which creates a sense of eternity, infinitude and transcendence.

the people around could be seen leaning reverently toward him.

I became rather bold and asked him what made him so popular. He responded good-naturedly, "Well, it's not really me, as such. You see, I am called a 'swami,' because I am a *sannyasi* (a renunciate). A sannyasi possesses nothing and is hence possessed by nothing. In one sense *sannyasa* means removing your own exclusive ego from your heart and calling in God, or say the highest value you can conceive, to sit there on the throne which was previously occupied by your ego." Then he told a story to illustrate the social impact of such a transformation:

There was once a boatman who each day would take his rowboat out into the lake to fish. Every evening when he returned to shore, he would tie his boat to the same tree. This went on for years. One day when he returned, he saw to his surprise that there was another boat tied to that particular tree. He walked up to it and looked in, but as nobody was there, he just shrugged his shoulders and tied his own boat to the next tree down the bank. The next day when he returned, the other boat was again there, and this time there was a man sitting in it. The first man became furiously angry and started howling and shrieking at the man sitting in the boat. Now, both days the situation of annoyance was exactly the same, but the first day the man had peacefully walked away, and the second day he became hysterical. Why? Because only on the second day was there a person in the other boat. "Like that, when you remove your ego from your boat, the other person will find it very easy to accept and adjust to you."

The practicalities of this process of abdication were to form the core of the initial teachings I was to receive from this man who seemed at once miles away and as accessible as my own thoughts. This was the man who, although he has always asked to be called simply by his name, "Nitya," was soon to be called "Guru" by thousands of people in and out of India.

15

Rejoining The Guru

I have now joined Guru's entourage in the middle of their "Gypsy Semester." The present troupe consists of five Malayalee (native to Kerala State) boys, three Malayalee girls and myself, plus dozens to hundreds who attend talks given at each new locale through which we travel. Except for a sixteen year old girl and me, all the regulars are in their twenties. For the first time in the fifteen years of my association with Guru, he is now occasionally mobbed by autograph seekers. I'm not sure if that is a good or bad sign. Guru (63) is recovering from a bad case of the flu, but seems generally strong, especially considering the demands made upon him.

My dear friend Jyoti is here and showing me the playfulness of a sister and the watchful care of a mother. She is a very attractive, though unselfconscious, Indian woman in her upper twenties. I have known her as a student and attendant of Guru for almost ten years. During this time I have marveled at how she can combine being both a serious student and a cut-up comedienne at the same time. I think Guru also appreciates her ability to make light of "heavy" situations and remain sober when others around her become raucous. She was the one to meet me yesterday when I flew into Cochin from Madras.

Two of the boys are great sports enthusiasts. It does my "jock" heart good to see them horse around and to watch the dance they went through to "sneak off" to find a T.V. for today's championship cricket match. One of them, Prince, shyly had me present his proposal to Guru for a Physical Education program to be added to Guru's East West University. The idea was readily endorsed.

In his lessons back in those first days when I was with Nitya, he talked a great deal about the inner tranquility necessary for a person's life to take on a lasting significance and harmony. Hatred, lust, and greed (and their accompanying fear, anger, and frustration) are the eternal stumbling blocks to such tranquility. If we look closely, we can see that it is desire which is always behind these emotions. For example, anger results from thwarted desire. Desires are a normal part of life, but how we tend to cultivate or minimize them and how we choose to act upon them will to a large measure determine our degree of inner peace.

In the West, desire and its gratification have been elevated almost to the status of a religion. Even the "quality of life" is most often measured by how wide-ranging and varied are the items of desire available. Spiraling desires and a clutter of potential gratifications are the hallmarks of modern society. This is the result of the "supply side" approach to dealing with the disturbance and dissatisfaction which accompany desire.

On the other side, Eastern traditions have sought peace through the attempt to moderate the demand rather than proliferate the supply. Hunger is satisfied by eating bland food just as much as if one had eaten tasty food. It follows that satisfaction is not from the object but from the cessation of the desire for it. Thousands of years ago the sages of India hypothesized that the natural state of the self is happiness, and that desire arises as a disturbance obstructing our natural state. Through detachment, nonpossessiveness, and in some cases asceticism, this hypothesis has been verified time and again.

Such a seemingly negative approach to self-fulfillment does not make life either barren or passive. In addition to clearly stating "The kingdom of heaven is within" (Luke 17:21), Jesus also promised, "Seek ye first the kingdom of heaven, and all else shall be added unto thee" (Luke 12:31). That "all else" becomes even a greater joy when it is appreciated as an elaboration or embellishment of the essential and inner basis of eternal joy. When personal desire based on a sense of deficiency is no longer our prime motivation, we become free to act on behalf of higher and more altruistic values.

When I first heard these ideas, they had a dramatic impact on the tenor and tempo of my inner life. My initial experience was an unburdening and a depressurization. I had been living in a state of chronic low-level anxiety over the uncertainty of what was to be my social niche in life and what was to be the source of my financial security. For the first time the projection and manipulation of *what could be* became secondary to a realization and understanding of *what is*.

At first, when the veils of fear and desire began to dissolve, I became perhaps even a bit intoxicated with the beauty and wonder of the ever-changing world of becoming and the eternal presence of an underlying pure being. As for the future, I knew only that I wanted it to stem from and be expressive of this dawning sense of peace and wonder.

Since rejoining Guru, so far we have stayed in a small new two-hut gurukula where I slept on the ground; in a rich man's house, sleeping on a bed under a fan; and now we are sleeping on the floor of a large meeting hall.

This morning I walked by myself (initially at least) to the beach and swam out into the Arabian Sea to an anchored fishing boat. I climbed up to sunbathe while nearly three dozen children whistled, hooted, waved and laughed from the shore. On the way back in, about fifty feet off shore, I reached with my feet to check for the bottom. To my horror and revulsion, instead of touching sand my feet sunk momentarily into a soft mushy goop that could only be decomposing excrement. Instantaneously a most pleasing outing became repulsive, and a seaside frolic became a reminder of the ever present dichotomy of the sublime and the vulgar which characterizes life in India. Hurriedly I floated back to shore, mentally canceling my plans for regular morning and evening swims the next three days while we're here.

Some undiminished pleasures have included banana *pulichery* (a sweet yogurt curry), more cold water bucket-and-dipper baths, daily tender coconut juice, numerous spicy dishes, and early risings before the onset of the sticky heat and mad commotions that characterize Kerala towns by day. On the pain side of the scale, my sciatic nerve continues to hurt, making sitting down problematic. Neither lying nor standing are acceptable in social settings here.

There are said to be forty-some varieties of bananas growing in Kerala. Each has its own distinct texture and flavor. This morning I sampled my two favorites. One is red on the outside and peach colored on the inside, and the other is pure white inside. Last night I had the kind that is green when ripe. I have heard that the Eskimos have thirty-five different words for "snow." Between forty varieties of "banana" and thirty-five types of "snow," one knows all one needs to know about the essential characteristic difference between the Arctic and Tropic regions of our home planet.

It is noteworthy that my backpack is holding up well, tipping the scales (not to mention my back) at forty five pounds. One of the Malayalee boys calls it my "mobile home," and indeed it is, with clothes for heat and cold, bedsheets, sleeping pad, book-lite, flashlight, dop kit and dipper, clothesline and five pins, vitamins, minerals and herbal remedies, cup, bowl and silverware, portable water purifier, camera, walkman, self-shiatsu acupressure board, books, notebook paper, ten disposable razors, money, a couple of plastic bags, the gifts I brought for friends here, and an elastic "bungy" cord to hold down automobile trunks that won't close around the whole lot when it is added to the luggage of others with whom I will be traveling.

I've been keeping a dream journal and am somewhat tickled and somewhat distressed to note that on three of the previous five nights I've had frustrated sports spectator dreams, oddly enough one for each "major" American sport. In one, Guru was teaching a class in my parents' dining room, and my father was watching an N.B.A. basketball game in the den. I went in to ask him to turn it down and was torn as to whether to stay and watch. A second night found me rerouting a flight to India through New Zealand, so I would have a layover at just the time of an N.F.L. football game I wanted to see on T.V. Last night I was on my way to a White Sox night double-header baseball game in the pouring rain.

In other dreams recently, I'm still on my way to India or the setting is part India, part America. I think some of this is due to the suddenness and radicalness of the change in environment, and some of it reflects certain resistance on my own part to let go of what is familiar, habitual and secure. I fully expect to catch up with myself soon.

This, to me though, is another sign that I should spend some time just sitting and meditatively watching the current tendencies of my mind and its favored associations, images, and fancies. I have found that bringing these into the light of conscious recognition does wonders in regard to reducing the unconscious sway they can otherwise hold over the entire psyche and its moods when they remain for the most part undetected.

I may be sitting at the feet of a great master, but even he can't do the work of meditation and reflection for me, any more than one person can eat a meal for another.

16

Man At Leisure God At Work

Today has been a deliciously slow day, sandwiched between two jokes. Last night was very long, as the Malayalee man named Ashok, who bedded down next to me on the floor, had the irritating habit of loudly groaning and grunting in his sleep several times a minute. By dawn (5AM), as we were getting up, I was curious to learn if he was aware of this trait.

I approached him and said, "All night long you were moaning and groaning."

He looked strained and asked, "What?"

"You—moaning and groaning," I said.

"What did you say?" he appealed.

"Moaning. Moaning," I repeated.

Relief flashed across his face, "Ah, yes, good moaning, Sir." And he walked away.

The second joke was my feeble performance on the volleyball court across the road this evening as our East West University crew challenged the local hot shots. This was my first attempt at a sport (due to my sciatica) in several months, and but for one stirring two-handed block of a monstrous "spike" at the net, my rustiness showed. Still, we didn't embarrass ourselves, as we only lost 15-13. One of their players competed superbly with malformed and crippled arms, more common on a beggar than a fine athlete.

On previous India visits I have found athletics to be a universal language capable of expressing goodwill and harmony. Once I stayed near a high school in New Delhi and on several occasions got to play with the team and their coaches. I particularly enjoyed the sense of mutual flow and dance, the blending of spontaneous movements with others whom minutes before were total strangers. I also very much appreciated the attitude of the Indian players who, as I would have predicted, were free of the hard edge of competitiveness which prevents one from recognizing and celebrating the successes and grace of one's "opponent." Whenever there was a particularly nice move or shot, the members of both teams were one in their expression of congratulations.

In between the good moaning and the nice evening, precious little happened after Guru's 6AM English dictation session. Guru never charges fees for his teaching or counseling. He feels that the wisdom which was passed along to him and the light of understanding that shines within him are a gift from some hidden source. He is grateful for his gift and figures that freely sharing it is the best way to express that gratitude. One way I have been able to reciprocate for all that he has done for me over the years is by helping take down, edit and type the books and articles that he writes. Previous collaborations, written and published during our travels together through India, Europe, the U.S., Fiji, Australia and Singapore, include the two books *Meditations on the Self* and *In the Stream of Consciousness*. His present project is a translation and commentary of Narayana Guru's "One Hundred Verses on Experiential Aesthetics and Imperiential Transcendence." The title itself merits a book-length commentary.

The following is part of what he had to say this morning:

> Living in the eternal present in itself indicates a very spiritual appreciation of life. If you can smile here and now with only that which is presently available, then life is lived to its fullest. Some people are sad because certain things are not present and sadder because other things are present. Two people can travel side by side, and one will be always happy and the other always sad. It is not the outer circumstances

but the clarity of their own reflecting mirror (their mind) which is the determining factor.

Once my father drew a portrait and then traced it on another sheet which he gave to my mother, brother, sister and myself to mark which part we felt was the most beautiful. One chose the eyes, one the hair, one the chin, one the lips. By the end each part had been selected. Later he handed us another copy asking us to mark what we thought to be the ugliest part. Naturally each part was again selected.

My father said, "Don't you see that everything is at once beautiful and ugly according to the subjective notions of the judge? When you look for ugliness, you will find it everywhere. When you look for beauty, you will find that everywhere. Brightness and darkness are attributes of our own consciousness."

6:00 AM is the only time Guru can squeeze in any English these days. During the rest of the day he is shuttled along with his retinue to and from four different functions in which he is the featured speaker. Dreading the Malayalam and the sciatic pain of prolonged sitting, I stay behind in his room, which has the only fan in the place. Outside it is hot enough to melt a candle.

This morning I read from Dogen's *Moon in a Dew Drop*, a book on Zen, and sat some zazen (meditation). Zazen involves a mindfulness practice in which one observes and dismisses each thought as it arises. As an aid to cultivating this vigilance that neither misses nor is distracted by anything, one is advised to simply count one's breaths from one to ten and then begin again at one. It is remarkable how difficult this simple task is to perform. Usually before one reaches four or five, one's mind has wandered off into some unsought memory or fantasy.

Sooner or later after the mind has begun to wander, one catches oneself and begins counting breaths again. This moment of catching oneself is a critical one. For just as Guru implied in the morning lesson, here too there are two possible responses to one's deviation from the task at hand. The first and most common is to feel frustration and anger with oneself, "Damn, I screwed up again." The second, equally valid and far more productive, is to feel actually proud, "Very good, I caught myself again. Now I can return to my practice." This latter approach can be carried over to our everyday life whereby even the discovery and recognition of a failure or shortcoming can itself become a success and a landmark on the road to self-development.

At one point this morning when I noticed my mind would not seem to slow down in spite of the peaceful atmosphere, I devised a little conundrum which proved to be an excellent inner conversation stopper:

> EXTRANEOUS THOUGHT
> When you think, are you not only thinking to yourself? Then what is it that you could possibly think to yourself that yourself would not already know?

Later in the morning I talked with a young Malayalee man who had stayed behind so he could speak with me about his drug addiction and fragile recovery. After four months of sobriety, he has finally gotten over the physical torment of withdrawals but is still suffering from wide mood swings and lack of concentration. As for the emotional swings, I shared with him the "secret" of even-temperedness which Guru's teacher, Nataraja Guru, had passed along to me:

> "Emotions will always fluctuate up and down to some extent. It is not possible to pull yourself up when you are feeling down. But if you want to get a handle on the process, it can be done by reining yourself in and restraining a bit when you feel yourself going high. That way when the inevitable down swing comes, it will go down *less* than it would have if you had let yourself get carried away in ecstasy. In any case there will be a balance, and if you want to soften the drastic quality of the swings, you can do so only by moderating the 'up' cycle."

His three word code for this technique was, "Don't shout 'hallelujah.'"

As for the trouble concentrating, I suggested that at this tender stage of his recovery, he needn't expect too much from his mind in this regard. It is not yet used to self-discipline. Rather than trying to maintain constant *concentration*, I suggested he should be satisfied if he could maintain constant *intention* for his recovery and continued self-development. At this stage that alone should guarantee success.

At midday I was visited by Sidharthan, an old friend from previous trips to India. Sidharthan is a handsome middle-aged businessman with a protruding paunch, which in India is a sign of affluence and good fortune. Unaware that the same plump belly in America symbolizes not affluence and good fortune, but rather a deficiency of fitness and self-will, Sidharthan loudly greeted me today with the implied compliment, "Mr. Peter, you have become quite fatty."

In the afternoon I spent hours reading through a book entitled *The Whys of a Philosophical Scrivener* by Martin Gardner, in which the former editor of "Scientific American" discusses many perspectives on such subjects as Prayer, Evil, and Immortality. For variety I read some in *The Great Railway Bazaar* by Paul Theroux, chronicling his journey by trains from London through Asia. I wrote a letter to my friend in Santa Rosa, Drow, who is planning to join me in January for one week in Kerala after his trek in Nepal. Of course, there was also time for rice, curry, and napping.

When Guru came back hot and tired between his third and fourth public talks of the day, I expressed sympathy. He responded, "So, you don't want to be a guru, then?" When I declined, Jyoti shared a story that Guru had told that very afternoon:

It seems Jesus and Peter were walking along a country road one morning. Peter was exclaiming the glory of God and speculated, "How I would love to be God even if just for one day."

Jesus remarked, "Better you start with a half day first."

Just then they came upon a woman who was tending a group of ducks. As they were passing, she put down her staff and started walking away. Jesus asked her, "Where are you going?"

She said, "I have a wedding to attend."

"But what about your ducks?"

"Oh, God will look after them," she said as she hurried off.

For the rest of the afternoon, Peter was chasing here and there trying to keep the ducks together with only minimal and short-lived success. After a few hours the woman returned and gathered up the ducks.

"So now what do you think?" Jesus asked Peter.

Peter answered, "Enough of this God business. I don't want it."

Three years ago, when last in India, I accompanied Guru to a remote town named Malayatoor. We visited the proposed site of a new gurukula on a finger of land laying between a rubber tree estate and a lake. At that time I had been very impressed with the peacefulness and beauty of the place.

Tomorrow Guru is sending me to this secluded lakeside retreat for ten days. While there I will receive treatment for my persistent sciatica pain at the healing hands of a famous *Ayurvedic* (ancient Indian science of health) physician who lives in the locality. The physician will come to the gurukula daily to administer special oil massages.

My desire to visit this gurukula increased when I learned the swami in charge is Anandan, my dear friend for thirteen years. We first met at the Bangalore Nature Cure Hospital where we were attending on Nataraja Guru during his final days. From that time onwards Anandan has been for me a model of good-natured and untiring service and devotion, lightened by humor and given weight by wisdom.

In the hospital Anandan slept on the floor at the foot of the Guru's bed. Each night before laying down, Anandan would adjust the crooked-neck table lamp sitting beside the

Guru's one functional arm. Anandan made sure the beam, when lit, would strike himself directly in the face and awaken him with a start. This method of calling would be used by the Guru numerous times each night for requests ranging from help getting onto the toilet to answers for questions such as, "What time is it?" and even once, "Where did they shoot George Wallace?" "I think it was Corvallis" was Anandan's half-wakeful yet immediate response, more out of the rhyme-logic of dream than out of any notion of veracity.

Thus when the promise of some significant treatment for my pain and disability is added to the allure of the setting and the pull of a good friend, my eagerness is strong enough to overcome my reluctance to leave Guru after traveling all this way to be with him. I will rejoin him in Trichur after ten days.

17

The Road
To Malayatoor

There is a touching ritual-like interchange that I periodically participate in with the simplest of Kerala natives. This is a sort of verbal dance in which the Malayalee, out of deference to me, speaks in a very basic broken English, and I, out of deference in return, speak my own form of pidgin Malayalam. Thus an entire conversation will take place in two languages, connecting almost as if by magic in a common meeting-ground of mutual human regard. One such conversation occurred this morning between myself and the conductor of a bus I had just boarded with my friend and escort, Babu. The conductor's words are in English, and mine are in Malayalam:

"Where going?"
"*Eniku Angamali pogunu. Etre pice?*"
"For two?"
"*Adai, runda.*"
"Twenty nine."
"*Eru pat umbata?*"
"Yes."
"*Sheddi.*"
"Thank you."

That bus ride was the first of three to eventually take Babu and myself to the Malayatoor Gurukula from where Babu continued on to his family's home which is also in Malayatoor. Babu is a young man in his early twenties, who seems to me to be traveling with Guru as much for the amusement and the social scene as for the teaching. His soft handsome features are further complimented by laughing brown eyes and a perpetual smile. In fact, the only times I have noticed that smile briefly evaporate are whenever I have attempted to speak to him. Each time he strains in vain, though with great sincerity, to understand me. But nothing in his meager training in English has prepared him to comprehend "American," and nothing whatsoever has prepared him to make sense of my feeble Malayalam. I suppose only the deaf and the well-traveled can know how satisfying a relationship can be which is based on grins, nods, and gestures. Once I gave up my attempts at verbal communication, his pearly white cheshire cat grin remained an uplifting constant.

Babu and I had risen at 5AM in order to travel and arrive in the cooler part of the day. In spite of this forethought, due to misinformation regarding bus schedules and the usual unprogrammed delays, we arrived at Malayatoor at midday and to the news that the one and a half miles of road to the lake were closed for repairs. We would have to walk.

The heat of the tropics at midday is itself like a weight. Added to this weight I hoisted upon my shoulders the backpack that was lightened slightly by the sense of irony that here I was on my way to have my weak back treated. I set my odds of success as comparable to those laid by Jesus on a camel passing through the eye of a needle or a rich man entering the kingdom of heaven. With each of my first few steps I said a silent thanks to Jyoti who had offered to take a parcel of some of my excess gear ahead with her to Varkala.

Soon my mind was taken up with the distractions of the road and roadside. Having no motor traffic on the road made the walk an uncommon pleasure. All along the way children would appear, running from the naturally camouflaged compounds within the jungle on either side of the road. As they came they would call back over their shoulders to alert their family and neighbors as to the passing show of the white man with the big load strapped on his back.

I have long recognized smiles as a universal solvent. I

noted again how, as usual, it is children who most naturally seem to radiate the joy of the spirit. Their smiles are felt in our own heart, and that reciprocity awakens the sense of our being One in that spirit and in that joy. When another person and I are smiling at each other, it is impossible to determine where my experience of the other's smile ends and my own smile begins or where the other's experience of my smile ends and his or her own smile begins and so on like that in one continuous upward spiral.

Mothers with their own wide smiles, holding babies on their hips, appeared at doorways. They would point and say something to their young ones—perhaps, "There is one of the *strange ones* we will send you to if you don't behave." In previous visits to India I have had such an ogre role cast upon me on buses and trains by clever mothers frustrated in their attempts to get their young children to behave.

We stopped at a couple of small shops along the way— literally "holes in the wall"—and purchased tiny bananas, wheat buns and cold bottles of mango soda pop from a refrigerator which looked at least a century ahead of its time in the dark hut with the dried cow-dung floor.

We passed the labor-intensive road crew in which the women carried baskets of rocks upon their heads and dumped them where the men distributed and beat them (the rocks!) into place. Between the women workers and myself there was a special smile of recognition acknowledging our respective loads.

Finally we reached the lake. Halfway around we came to the gurukula. Anandan Swami greeted us with a quiet unflappable joy. He had not received Guru's letter announcing my arrival and had been planning to leave the next day for Varkala. Had we arrived one day later, the gurukula would have been locked and abandoned. With the ease and cheer characteristic of *ananda* (the blissful nature of the self), he now changed his program in order to remain with me for ten days and then accompany me with Guru to Varkala. I could hardly wait to plunge in the lake. By the time I returned, a pot of rice was bubbling on a wood and coconut husk fire.

18

Wealth Beyond Money

The dawn here is signaled by both a bang and a whimper. The bang occurs even before the first hint of light, as the profound silence is shattered by the blaring of screeching music through a scratchy loudspeaker from the church across the lake. The whimper, of course, is mine as I am violently jolted from one state of consciousness to another. Unfortunately, one can't even blame the missionary zeal that characterizes much of Christianity worldwide for this rude intrusion. In fact, the Christians are simply adopting a modern tradition followed by temples and mosques the length and breadth of the Indian subcontinent.

It is a testimony to the adaptability of the human psyche that one soon learns to accept, ignore or even appreciate this obnoxious cacophony, associating it with the miracle of a new day by which it is always followed. Still I have found that each of the seven times I have come to India, it has taken me awhile to adjust to this aspect of Indian life.

Unlike most of Kerala, it gets quite cool here at night. I start out going to bed without even a sheet. After several nights here I have come to mark the night's progression in terms of temperature rather than time, as in "half past socks" or "quarter to jacket."

At about "twenty past music" the sky begins to faintly lighten. Without even raising my head off the pillow, I can see the outline of a mountain reflected in the gently glowing lake, the shore of which begins less than fifty feet from our hut.

At the first crimson blush of the sky, the swami and I get up and begin the day. As he goes down to the little stream to wash out the two pots used to cook the previous evening's *cungi* (rice gruel) and curry, I make several trips to the well, drawing and carrying the water for the day's kitchen and latrine needs. Then as I spread out a bamboo mat in the courtyard to do some gentle therapeutic yoga exercises for my back, the swami sweeps up the dust and sand and sweeps out the ants that have gathered overnight in the prayer-hall and on the veranda. He is very apologetic about disturbing the ants, who as he says, "after all were here before we came and have every right to feel that human beings are pests and a general nuisance."

Shortly after 7:00 the *vaidyar* (Ayurvedic physician) comes walking with a youthful bounce uncharacteristic of a man of his years (mid-sixties). He is very dark-skinned, round-faced, balding with white hair around the sides and back of his head, and very thin. Generally serious and reverent, his periodic bright smiles burst forth with the intimation of a joy that remains for him an inner constant rather than being an alternating pleasure principle which spends itself and then requires time and circumstance to favor renewal.

During our walk in, we had stopped at his shop, and he had offered to come to the gurukula to see me that very afternoon. I was amazed to find that from his hands-on diagnosis he was able to tell me (through Swami's translation) everything I had been experiencing with my back. I mentioned only that I had some acupuncture treatments after surgery, and with his thumb he located the exact meridian from which the pain had been removed. After some more exploration he proclaimed that while diverting the energy from that area, the acupuncture itself had created a blockage on the other side which was partially responsible for my present pain and disability. He pinpointed where the circulation was very sluggish, where various nerves were contracted, and specific muscles inoperative. He then proceeded to give me the first in a series of oil massages.

After the first treatment I found I could sit with about 20% less pain, and after the second I noticed similar relief when rising from sitting, which is the major problem. This relief has increased day by day as has my flexibility.

The vaidyar must walk a half hour each way to come and return home. All he seems to require by way of reward is my satisfaction. After he finishes, he sits on the veranda, and we give him a piece of fruit, a bun or a couple of cookies, and a cup of tea or herbally medicated water. Before coming I asked Guru if the vaidyar would tell me what I owed him and if not what and when I should pay him. Guru laughed and said, "Anyway, he won't ask for anything, but if you like, when you say good-bye to him for the last time, you can look into his eyes, smile, and hand him 100 rupees (about $8)." When he saw me wince and grimace, Guru said, "Alright, if you have enough to spare, you can give him 200 rupees" (this for ten days of message and travel time!).

Now, I have met this vaidyar and have been the recipient of his selfless service and benefactor of his hard-earned talent. I am humbled almost to the point of mystification. He neither expects comparable return for his labors in any material sense, nor does he particularly care for it.

I feel very small-minded and primitive when I think how much we Americans are raised and encouraged to be motivated by the desire for financial or material gain. Moreover we actually evaluate the worth of contributions between ourselves and others in terms of money given or money received. In fact, this system regulating human transaction is so deeply ingrained as to almost appear self-evident. It is only upon encountering a culture or individual who embodies a completely different frame of reference for self-motivation, self-evaluation, and human transaction that we are shocked into the realization that what we hitherto took for granted as simply "the way things are" is only a culturally conditioned pattern of belief and behavior.

My ideas of wealth and poverty have undergone radical

redefinition since my exposure to India and her people. Abundance, affluence, and opulence are three grades of reality which call for reevaluation. In some sense they could be said to represent respectively the natural, the sophisticated, and the pompous. Without bank accounts or even heavily stocked larders, the Indians I have met have a sense of being the recipients of Nature's abundance day after day. Their feeling of the sufficiency of Nature's provision expresses itself in the attitude of there being always enough extra to share.

More than once when I thought I was only being frugal with my reserves, Guru has pointed out what he calls a "poverty consciousness" in my hesitation to let my money flow outwards (I will have occasion to go into Guru's economic theories and practices in greater detail later). An essential ingredient in the fostering of wealth or poverty, often overlooked in the West, was declared thousands of years ago by the Chinese philosopher, Lao-Tzu, who proclaimed, "He who knows he has enough is a rich man." Such an insight is not to be used to perpetuate the oppression of others, but rather to facilitate the promotion of oneself. Think about it.

19

The World In The Self

From the time the vaidyar leaves (around 8:00AM) until 9:00AM, I have been making a hand copy of the dictations Guru gave me last week to send to Vinod, the manager of the gurukula in Ooty, for him to enter and print on the new computer there. At 9:00 the swami and I sit for prayer, meditation, chanting and reading. At the end of one such session the swami, who is tirelessly active throughout the day, proclaimed, "There. At least now we have done something truly useful."

The following passages from our readings this week (from Narayana Guru's *One Hundred Verses of Self-Instruction* — commentary by Nataraja Guru, verses 3-5) may give a flavor of their rich content and a peep into the contemplative foundation of the Indian world-view:

> The world of appearance is only the specific aspect of the basic consciousness in which all things have being. Name and form are the factors giving specificity to the general consciousness.
> Just as the trained scientist can understand wave mechanics in terms of Max Planck's constant "h," so the philosopher is asked here to look at the successive grades of phenomenal manifestation of the visible world as substantially the same as the stuff of consciousness itself.
> There is a subtle tri-basic factor which is responsible for our wrong appraisal of reality. The lazy mind left to itself without the attitude of contemplation has a tendency to view

reality from an angle that takes for granted the knower, knowledge as a concept, and the objective side of knowledge as three distinct entities. In order to apprehend reality and become liberated from the snares of life, one has to counteract this prejudice to which the human mind is naturally disposed.

[This calls to mind the insight of the Western psychologist Fritz Perls encapsulated in his statement, "Whereas the sentence, 'I see a tree,' can indeed be divided into subject and object, in the actual experience no such division exists.]

The identity of subject and object as the central doctrine of contemplative life and wisdom generally has been recognized both in the East and the West. The reference of Plotinus to contemplation as "the flight of the alone to the Alone" is a direct paraphrase of the state of *kaivalya* (aloneness or all-oneness) which is the goal of contemplation according to Indian schools.

...Plurality of interests and thoughts arising from desires or instinctive hungers that cannot be wholly satisfied are the enemy of the contemplative. This does not mean, however, that to be a contemplative means killing out the legitimate joys of life. But in and through all interests a master interest must always be preserved. All actions and thoughts motivating them must be gathered together into a master life-tendency so verticalized as never to conflict with the minor fissiparous dissipating interests of a life without such a dominating interest. What is here implied is a process of sublimating pluralistic interests to a unitive interest.

Nataraja Guru, who wrote the above passage, was Guru Nitya's teacher, and is thus my "grandguru." When I met him during the last years of his life, he was a short-statured, long-bearded, plump, impish man whom his Western students referred to as "Mr. Natural" because of his resemblance to the comic book character of that name. His passion was the integration of modern science with religion, philosophy, and art in such a way so as to leave no area of human endeavor outside the pale of our highest aspirations for creative fulfillment, penetrating understanding, and lasting happiness. His *magnum opus* is a thousand plus page book entitled *An Integrated Science of the Absolute*.

Although I listened to many of his lectures, I did not often approach him personally. Once I did approach him and asked how to meditate. His quick and unexpected reply was, "Meditate on the world without you in it." Fifteen years later I am still using that seemingly off-the-wall suggestion as a periodic theme for meditation while active as well as inactive. I find such an exercise can be both clarifying and unburdening. The field of interest swells becoming Life itself and is no longer constricted to the stifling arena of *my* life. The subject matter and object matter of such a meditation fuse in such a way that it is (I am) just Life being Life, Life contemplating Life, and Life loving Life. From such a perspective even my own personal death is no more nor less significant than that of a leaf falling from a tree.

Along this same line, I recently read about a wonderful dialogue between a guru and his student. The guru had been speaking about liberation, and the student interrupted, "What do you mean by liberation?" The guru replied, "Freedom from the 'I.' " The student, being very clever, protested, "But if there is no 'I,' then who is free." To which the immediate response was, "The world is free of a mighty nuisance. That's good enough."

After "Prayer" I gather up my dirty clothes from the day before, a book, a mat, sunglasses and cap, towel, bathing and laundry soap and walk 100 feet down to the lake to wash clothes, sunbathe, lakebathe, read and swim. Sunbathing is unknown in India, and the sun is avoided at all costs. Umbrellas are pressed into service even more often for shade than for shielding against the rain. Thus whenever an Indian sees me supine in the direct sun, the immediate assumption is that either I have fallen down in a faint or else I am mad. Frequently they will come close and discovering it is not the former, go on their way satisfied it is the latter.

Baking on the warm rocks after soaking in the cool water sends me into a pleasant dreamy state. On my first morning down by the lake, I notice that something seems to be wrong with me. At first I'm puzzled. What more could I possibly ask for? Then I notice what it is. There is an ache in my heart, a sense of emptiness or loss. Oh yes, I still haven't gotten over the separation from Carolyn. I miss her. The thought of missing her triggers a red flag.

Suddenly I am transported back to a walk I took with Guru over ten years ago when we were visiting my parents in Illinois. He remarked that I seemed a little "down" that morning. I casually mentioned that I missed a certain girlfriend whom I hadn't seen for a few months. His response took me by surprise:

"You shouldn't treat people as objects of your enjoyment. The degree that you miss someone when they are not physically presented to your senses, is the degree that you view that person as an object. This is the seed of all exploitation. Not only is that person most precious as their own subjective self which neither increases nor decreases, but beyond that this person now constitutes a beloved facet of your own subjective self, which also knows no coming nor going within itself. Thus by 'missing' them, you are doing both of you a grave disservice. It is this same basic error of objectification, which is behind 'missing' someone, that is also at the root of all oppression, exploitation and much interpersonal conflict."

Those words remain with me today as the echo of a shock therapy which forever put me on the alert to the subtle and gross ways in which I and other people tend to treat others as objects. The real affirmation that these ideas constitute more than an intellectual exercise came on one of the most trying nights of my life. I was in Europe traveling and studying with Guru and helping him work on the book he was writing when I received the news that my girlfriend of longstanding had drowned in a rafting accident.

The news hit me like a knife in the gut. That following night I spent in communion with her in dream and in meditation. Then, more than ever, I wanted to grasp the implications of Guru's words about the union of subject and object.

I was surprised at how easily I could feel her unique "vibration" which I had come to cherish over the years. It occurred to me that so long as I had thought of her as external, it had only been with much planning and effort in the past couple of years that we had been able to bring ourselves to and continue in each other's presence. Although now she was no longer anywhere in particular, I had a sense that she was equally everywhere in general. I then realized experientially that ultimately what we love in another person is a particular tuning of our own "heart-strings" which that person's presence brings about in us.

Recalling all this lying on the rocks by Malayatoor Lake, I realized 'missing' Carolyn was indeed evidence of her presence within me rather than her absence. The ache did not vanish, but it was somehow consoling to be able to identify and honor that ache itself as one fragmentary facet of the unit "Carolyn and Peter," within me. Thus, projected absence was converted into dynamic presence, and the ache itself became a source of enrichment.

20

Like Rays Of Sun

Each day when I return to the gurukula from the lake, we prepare our midday meal. I take satisfaction in cutting "vegetables" such as green mango, green banana, lady's finger (okra), drumsticks, onions, garlic, tomatoes, cabbage, green beans, etc. for curries. Swami prepares them either into thick soupy *sambars* or dry *torens* with grated coconut. Curry leaves and green chilies are constants, as of course is the red-flecked white rice which we have dry for lunch and served as gruel in the evening.

Lunch is usually followed by two bananas and one nap. The siesta is often cut short by the shouts and laughter of the neighborhood children who come almost daily to the gurukula for free English and math tutorials from the swami. Studying easily slips into games of hop-tag or catch with a ball ingeniously woven from palm fronds. These games are accompanied by the universal language of glee which is the special province of childhood.

An older boy who also comes, named Thomas, wanted to test out his English on me. What came out, from Heaven knows where, was, "Yesterday I bathroom. Today you bathroom. Is it correct?" Not wanting to open a can of worms or worse, my quick reply was, "Yes, it is very correct."

Sitting on the tile and brick veranda of the gurukula, one can watch a languid procession of brahma bulls, cows, water buffalo, lean dogs and goats. Many stop and stand as if at a traffic light or in deep meditation before moving on. The impression is of some silent bovine version of "Mother May I" with the Mother operating as an inner controlling principle. Snow white cranes, jet black crows and shocking blue kingfishers add an aerial dimension to the spectacle.

All spiritual search has at its core two questions, "Who am I?" and "Whence this world?" To ponder on the first question is called a "meditation of self-inquiry." When I was first living with Guru, he gave me some guidelines to help me become more familiar with four aspects of my self:

1) Each of us has a physical existence which has an extension in space. It is concrete, objective, and subject to direct perception. He suggested I attempt to apprehend just what aspects of the total "I" belong to this category of our physical nature.

2) Next I was to think of everything which is of the nature of awareness or consciousness in me. This, of course, includes as much of the first category as I can be aware of plus much, much more. My consciousness penetrates into the vast cosmos around me, which in turn gets into my consciousness. My awareness of vital urges, emotions, and philosophical theories is also included here.

3) When I felt I'd nearly exhausted these two categories, I was to think of that which is of the nature of the "light" within me, that universal and eternal principle which animates my physical being and illuminates my conscious being. This takes me beyond the phenomenal to an experience of the noumenous within me. That is neither the object seen nor the subject which is the seer (both of which are fleeting) but that eternal vision which is the mysterious middle term bringing about the blissful union of the seer and the seen.

4) Finally I was to meditate on that aspect of my being which is of the nature of sacrifice. Here I could think of all the levels at which something in me is burnt up, consumed, or offered up as a sacrifice to the Absolute. Depending on my frame of mind, I found this could include such things as

the physical body, external actions, vital urges, emotions, social values, intellectual items, psychic and intuitive factors, as well as my very spirit itself.

In pondering these facets of the self over a period of days and weeks, I discovered that even my moment to moment sense of identity and presence was undergoing a transformation. For me the most dramatic change was in regard to the fluctuating physical and emotional states which previously occupied the majority of my attention. After the meditations these seemed more like "storms in a teacup." My perspective widened, and I began paradoxically to identify with all that was around me and at the same time to detach my sense of well-being from dependence on any of the ever-shifting variables of the phenomenal world. Equanimity or sameness in pain and pleasure, and praise and blame is both a strict requirement and sweet fruit of yoga (at once means and end). Only when my self-identity transcended my body and ego was such an equanimity possible.

Naturally what we identify as our "self" largely determines what we will consider necessary for our self-happiness. Our life energy goes mostly into those parts of our being and personality with which we identify. Almost constantly, various aspects of our total being are, so to speak, calling out in an attempt on the part of each to claim the role of "self" for itself and hence to dominate our pursuit of happiness. For example, when we say, "I am cold" or "I am hungry," the "I" refers to or is identified with the body. When we say, "I am angry" or "I like you," usually the self is identified with the emotions and the social ego. When we say, "I am confused" or "I think this is correct," the "I" means the mind or intellect.

But is the true self any of these demanding rival claimants (body, senses, mind, intellect, ego)? Or is there something which stands equally above all of these as a witness, which can say "my body," "my mind," "my emotions," "my intellect"? What is the nature and extent of that pure witnessing awareness? That was to become the focal point of my search for self-realization.

At dusk we once again bathe and cool ourselves at the lake before sitting for our evening "Prayer" session. Afterwards we eat our simple evening meal of rice served in its own water and either curry leftover from noon or a new one prepared fresh.

With the dinner over, a day that was already mellow seems to slow down one more notch. Usually I take a short or long stroll, with Swami or alone, around the lake, pausing to marvel, looking down at the entire skyful of stars shimmering up from the glassy surface of the lake. During one such instance I remained transfixed. Exactly what was shimmering—the stars? the sky? the earth's atmosphere? the lake? my mind? or the Consciousness of God? On another occasion Swami and I stood awestruck by the display of a supernova (an exploding solar system) flashing red-blue-green-yellow above the mountain across the lake.

I value my friendship with Anandan Swami perhaps beyond any other I have cultivated in India. He is dear to me as a precious aspect of my own self, and I in turn feel proud to be in some way an extension of him. Our friendship is not of the ordinary social variety. Our sharing is beyond the personality level.

I am reminded of something I was told by a Westerner staying at the Gurukula when I first arrived there in 1971. He suggested, "A gurukula is not so much concerned with looking one another in the eye as it is with fixing the gaze of all in the same direction." The direction leads at first inward to the spirit which is at the core of one's self. Then only after this self becomes familiar, can we clearly look outward and see that very same self radiating, at slightly different frequencies, through the eyes of all. Relationships thus become vertical rather than horizontal. All horizontal relationships, no matter how close, are subject to comings and goings and vulnerable to endless misunderstandings and disagreements. Vertical relationships rather than dealing with personalities and common external interests, anchor themselves to the unchanging self in all and in this way are assured of enduring.

Anandan Swami, bless his heart, reserves his love for no one in particular and everyone in general. His brilliant eyes beam like the sun, and like the sun they shine equally on all. It is an ironic and unappreciated fact that the closer one gets to one's own source, the selfsame source of all, the closer one will be to all others also. Rays of the sun are closest to one another when closest to their source.

Another evening I got out my walkman and circled the lake to the accompaniment of the sweet sounds of Mark Knopfler's soundtracks from the films "Local Hero" and "Cal."

Other evening sounds are husband/wife arguments heard in stereo from the huts behind the gurukula and across the lake. Swami explains that drinking is the source of the problem. There is very little work available in this locality— some seasonal work in the paddy fields, some wood gathering in the forest, minimal fishing in the lake. In idleness and low self-esteem the men turn to liquor, becoming abusive or targets for abuse or both.

On the other side of the lake is the dormitory and rehearsal hall for a traveling temple band. The instruments include drums of many sizes, large cymbals, and various horns, some four or five feet long. Rehearsals often go on until two in the morning. It is sometimes comical, sometimes thrilling, sometimes aggravating, and sometimes disorienting to hear over and over again a few short bars, of what in its totality must be a grand performance, arise out of silence and abruptly end, repeated *ad nauseum*.

Somehow, whether in sweet silence or familiar cacophony, sleep seems to come early and easily, as the conscious light dims, yielding to dreams of homes gone by, friends, family, strangers, and adventures too true to be real.

21

When Heaven Goes To Hell

Implying that a number of days are alike, as I did in my most recent journal entries, is as naive and prejudicial as claiming "All Chinese look alike." Last month in Singapore a Chinese waitress continued to insist I had been in her restaurant one week before, in spite of my assurances I had been in Honolulu (All Caucasians rook arike).

There is a germ of truth in my lumping a number of days together. I have noticed, during several visits to the tropics, the development of certain underlying rhythms, providing repetitive backdrops against which each day presents an entirely unique melody. I suppose this to be true everywhere and only experience it most keenly in tropical climes.

One of my days here was so dramatically different that even the rhythm was drastically affected. My third day here dawned with a sore throat and runny nose. Before noon my sinuses had flared and swelled to almost bursting. The same world, which the day before appeared as a paradise, now contracted into a single tight angry throb. The children's sweet voices became an irritating nuisance, and even the kind swami was transformed into a shadow to be avoided. There was nothing to do but lay on my bed and suffer.

At one point I overheard the swami apologetically justifying my mood to some visitors. In the midst of a Malayalam explanation, there suddenly came the English word "gloomy." Even that word became a source of aggravation to me. I thought to myself, "These incorrigible Malayalees. They are so damn cheerful, they don't even have their own word for 'gloomy.' "

How slight the difference between heaven and hell! It is no wonder Jesus proclaimed, "The kingdom of heaven is within." I am now of the belief that, given one's physical health, one ought to be able to find at least some heavenly virtues in any setting. And for those highly attained ones, a club into which I cannot yet claim membership, poor health itself need not be a barrier.

As with their approach to happiness, Indians also have a dramatically different approach to pain and suffering than we do in the West. Once when I was living with Guru in Portland, Oregon, where he was teaching at the University, he had a bad toothache. Although the pain was not unbearable, it was annoying enough to keep him from sleeping. At 3:00 in the morning I heard someone rattling around in the kitchen, and I went down to investigate. There was Guru blending together a number of herbs, such as sage, ginger, and cayenne and boiling them in water, which he then gargled.

"Does that reduce the pain?" I asked innocently.

"No," he grimaced, "It intensifies the pain for five agonizing minutes, and then the aggravation completely disappears."

I learned that the theory behind this phenomenon is that pain and suffering, be it physical, emotional, mental, psychic or spiritual, is the inevitable fruit of one or another transgression from the normal harmonious functioning at one of these levels. Hence the Indian approach is not to try to escape from or put off the inevitable. If x amount of pain is to be suffered, then they would rather get it over with than to have it drag on for long periods of time. This does not condone self-inflicted pain which can be a large transgression from harmony. Yet many Indians almost welcome pain, seeing it as the voice of some deep-seeded inner seer warning them about their deviations from their true nature.

Another time, in Australia, a radio interviewer asked Guru how his philosophy affects the way in which he looks at and reacts to suffering. I transcribed his reply:

"Suffering and its positive counterpart, compassion, belong to the necessary aspect of life. Suffering neither should nor can be avoided. I have had many opportunities to witness my reaction to personal tragedy in my own life and more often in the lives of people very dear to me. In suffering and personal tragedy, I always look for the element of the unseen all-knowing hand of God, the Tao, or the Absolute. Often the suffering contained a warning about certain schemes, attitudes, or patterns of behavior. Often the suffering or tragedy by, so to speak, closing one door actually necessitated a change in direction. Usually in retrospect it then appeared as if a very benevolent hand had been at work. You see there is something greater than the desires of each of us as an individual. Often our desires may clash with a Greater Will. Then we have what we call suffering. If you set your sights on this most high or absolute value, suffering will be minimized if not eliminated."

For my own part this philosophy has helped me distinguish a difference within myself between pain and suffering. Pain is a fact. Physically it is the inevitable result of the agitation of certain nerves. Emotionally it is the inevitable outcome of cherishing certain habits, attachments, and preferences. I have come to see suffering, on the other hand, as a resistance to pain. Thus it has become a goal of mine to accept (though certainly not cultivate) pain and to minimize suffering.

I have made some progress in this regard on an emotional level, for example enduring as inevitable the pain coming from the disillusionment of my marriage. The suffering intensifies greatly when I fall into resisting rather than bearing with this pain. As my day in "hell" attests, I cannot report as much progress *vis a vis* my acceptance of physical pain. I'm working on it.

The following day my sinuses cooled down, and I asked Swami Anandan, "Is this the same place where I was yesterday? Am I the same man who was lying here then?" Neither of us could adequately explain the transformation.

22

The Luxury Of Simplicity

During my nine days here, we have ventured away from the lakeside community only twice, both times to take the half hour, six cent bus ride into Kalady, the nearest big town. The trips were prompted by the need for a bank, post office, stationary store and fruit & vegetable market, but the highlight of each escapade was the full-course vegetarian meal at the tiny restaurant called Lakshmi Vilas Bhavan.

For three and a half rupees each (27 cents) we were served, on a banana leaf plate, all we could eat of rice, sambar, hot mango pickle, two tasty vegetable curries, *papadams* (large potato-chip-like delicacies), yogurt, buttermilk (which is actually milk from which all the butter has been removed) and spicy *rasam* (a soup of tomato, garlic, pepper and spices). The quality is comparable to Gaylord's, the fine Indian Restaurant in San Francisco, where a meal of significantly smaller quantity would cost *fifty* times the amount.

Once after finishing a similar meal in an Indian restaurant, Guru asked me, "Which country has greater wealth, India or America?"

Wary of some kind of trap, I still answered, "America."

He asked, "How much would you pay to eat a meal like this in America?"

I replied, "At least $8.00."

"Right, and in India this same amount of food can be had for $.25." Then he asked, "Do you know what accounts for price variations?"

"The main factor is supply and demand," I suggested.

At which point Guru said, "That's right. The demand for food is a constant, but the supply can vary. The fact that America has to charge you $8.00 for this amount of food which India can afford to give you for 25 cents suggests to me an abundance or wealth in India which is more fundamental than financial currency."

This was one blow to my preconceived notions of wealth and poverty which my experience in India and with Indians has forever altered.

My concept of "luxury" has also undergone a radical transformation. I now think one of the greatest luxuries is the luxury of simplicity. For the past ten days I have been enjoying the tropical "luxury" of no electricity and no running water. Luxuries usually consist of conveniences, and this one affords us the ultimate convenience of tuning our days to Nature's Rhythms and Reasons: rising and retiring with the sun, drawing water from the well, cooking our simple meals over wood and coconut husk fires, bathing in the lake, sharing knowledge and laughter with children. All of this seems most convenient given a minimum of artifice and technological sophistication.

Having to draw and carry water then used for bucket baths, laundry-by-hand, latrine flushing, cleaning, boiling for drinking, and cooking over hand-fed wood fires is all very time consuming. Yet the profoundly natural purposefulness of time spent attending to such necessities ironically increases the depth of leisure and contentment one feels throughout the rest of the day.

Isn't it paradoxical how all the labor-saving devices in the West, which tend to make dealing with the necessities of life seem trivial if not vaguely irrelevant, indirectly contribute to a chronic restlessness, a sense of rudderlessness and, in some, even worthlessness? Most of us in the West have lost touch with the gloriously direct and yet mysteriously spiritual implications of the Earth, the Water, the Fire, the Air, and the vast "Quarters of Heaven," which not only give us birth, but also support, sustain, protect, connect, and inspire us right in our daily lives as we go about the business of survival on the one hand and the creative expression of our inner wealth on the other hand.

One afternoon I was alone weeding in the gurukula potato fields. I became inexplicably filled with a sense of the intensity of love I felt from the Earth for all of us, her creatures. I was humbled by the tiny, almost negligible, service I was able to do for her by way of appreciation and adoration. The work was not enjoyable in the common sense of the word, but my heart was in it to the point of overflowing. I was washed by a wave of the Earth's unconditional benevolence with which she works night and day to turn mud into food.

I realized that my present mood of reverence, adoration, and duty, or rather "belongingness," was in my experience a characteristically Indian disposition. I wondered why it is so uncommon in the West and why it has taken me so long to come to it. Is it partially because we walk on concrete and, more to the point, because we get our food, the fruit of the Earth, in supermarkets? When I was a child, I actually thought food was manufactured or fabricated much like other industrial goods. In my adult life I have been surprised to learn that many others also grew up with the same impression. If at all we feel gratitude, given such a delusion, it is not to the Earth but rather is likely to be to the corporations and industries that intervene between her benevolence and us. Our primary sentiment for her soil, which is behind the miracle of food, is reflected in our characterization of it as "dirty!"

This is not to imply that when in India I don't sometimes long for a hot running shower or a washing machine or that I haven't frequently cursed my ineptitude at keeping a wood cooking fire burning at the appropriate level. What I do want to suggest is that there seems to be a direct correlation between peace of mind as well as creative inspiration and the groundedness that comes through dealing immediately rather than mediately (i.e. via the mediation of machines and devices) with the necessities of life. My guess is that the crucial factor is more attitudinal than behavioral. It would be possible, for example, to pause before one turns on a washing machine to give thanks for the rain. Without such reflection, this nourishing and cleansing rain strikes us primarily as an inconvenience (bad weather?).

Westerners, in general, also have difficulty accepting the Indian proposition that the inmost nature of our own self is characterized by peace and well-being and that nature outside also tends toward a state of harmonious peace. Making our way through a flood of automobiles, televisions, radios, bulldozers, air hammers and roaring crowds, many understandably cannot believe Nature always tends toward a state of harmony. Walking on concrete in the shadow of buildings, many people gather their information regarding Nature from the media, which will on every given day manage to expose the one flood, hurricane, earthquake, or natural calamity occurring in one village, province or town out of the world's million provinces.

Thus, the saying, "You are what you eat" has a significance for consumption in general and not just physically. Of course physically our entire body, from the toenails to the cells of the brain, having grown from a tiny sperm, is nothing other than the transformed matter of every tomato, apple, onion, pig, chicken or bull that we have eaten. This is literally so.

We do not live by bread alone. Matter is not the only thing we consume so we may transform and grow. Our senses too are continuously feasting on the world around us. When we see a great mountain peak or a pastoral setting, our whole inner being seems to resonate with the grandeur and serenity of the vision. When we perceive violence, commotion, or chaos, our mind and entire psycho-physical organism becomes agitated and disturbed. Sweet fragrances can put a radiant smile on our face, and unpleasant odors can make us grimace and become very ugly. Certain rhythmic sounds can make us dance, whereas certain pitches can grate upon our nerves and make us wince.

Our social nature feeds on emotions. Our intellect, for its growth, rejects visibles in favor of the consumption of ideas.

Our psyche is fed by intuitions and messages from hidden channels. Our spirit, or deepest self, is ever being fed from the divine source of life, light and well-being.

Thus what we seek and permit ourself to consume has a dramatic effect on who we are, how we perceive the world, and perhaps most important of all, how we reflect who we are and the world we perceive through our ongoing acts of creative self-expression. The two poles between which all life eternally swings are consumption and creation. What we consume determines what we shall be. What we are will determine what we create. It is said that even God's creation of "man" was in His (sic) own image.

Just as a lake can only contain a finite amount of the infinite supply of water, an individual human life in order to take on significance must discriminate and set limitations and make priorities among the multitudinous sources of potential nourishment. Although I feel reflection on the types and nature of nourishment sought and their impacts can be valuable for everyone, the process has a particular poignancy for me at this point in my life. When my wife presented me with her list of criticisms and grievances before our separation, "preoccupation with entertainment" was included.

When my initial defensive reaction to that accusation wore off, I was able to examine it with a clearer head. I was forced to realize that indeed I had begun to devote an inordinate amount of energy to seeking out, planning on, preparing for, and enjoying diversions such as sports, movies and concerts. None of these activities are bad in and of themselves. In fact, they are capable of providing relaxation, education, and inspiration. But in my case I can now see that when given an exaggerated degree of importance, they do indeed become diversions *from*, rather than contributors *to*, my primary goals and values.

The simplicity of my surroundings and activities these past ten days have again afforded me the luxury of coming back to a communion with the inner and outer nature which produces, sustains, and ultimately unites us all. Such communion leads to a pattern of consumption which is much more likely to contribute to the type of creativity which may be of significance to others.

The vaidyar has increased his treatments to two each day, giving a full body massage in the morning and concentrating on the legs in the afternoon. This he did cheerfully and with neither external inducement nor reward. Also he now incorporates a "foot massage" into both sessions. I don't mean he massages my feet, which he regularly does also, but rather he massages me with his foot. Supporting himself with both hands holding a rope looped over a rafter, he can apply varying degrees of pressure as he moves his well-oiled foot up and down my body. The "laying on of feet," as it were.

By now the pain is reduced by 50% and is experienced primarily when stretching to touch my toes from a sitting position. He is also fine-tuning the right leg which was operated on, and he has brought almost full range of motion back to the knee which my surgeon told me I would probably never be able to bend fully again.

Today marks the conclusion of this ten day retreat. Tomorrow I will be meeting Guru in Trichur to begin an intensive month-long session of traveling and studying with him. The quietude and solitude of the Malayatoor Gurukula has allowed me to once again open my heart which had become constricted and sore from my recent losses. I feel this openness of heart is the ideal condition in which to approach Guru. The light and love he radiates may be received and find an echoing response of regeneration within me. Soon I should begin to get an idea of how well the peace and insights derived during these ten days translate into the so-called "real" world, if that is how one can refer to the phantasmagoria that constitutes life in India.

23

An Atheist Goes To Temple

Today I was presented with a good insight into the Indian psyche:

I came to Trichur two days ago via a three hour, three bus ride accompanied by both Swami and Vaidyar. We came to meet up with Guru, who took the six hour train ride up from Varkala to inaugurate a temple function.

Our host here is Dr. Raja Mohan, a veterinary doctor and college professor. He is an avowed and proud "non-believer," free-thinker, atheist. Yet this morning when we were left behind after Guru's departure to the function (I, in order to avoid the three hours of Malayalam speeches and Dr. Mohan, because of later work commitments), his one suggestion was that I might like to visit the famous local Hindu temple.

Ordinarily I pass up such opportunities, just as was my custom with museums in Europe. This may very well be a sign of an overly prosaic mind, but be that as it may, I have long since renounced feigning interest where none naturally stirs. In this case however my curiosity was piqued by the possibility of an atheist's eye view of a Hindu temple.

In the daily worship of the Indian, regardless of the particular faith expressed, one can again see the characteristic difference between their approach to life and ours. In India prayers of thankfulness preponderate over prayers of petition. Cultivating gratitude for what one has is the inverse of cultivating ways to acquire what one has not. It is no wonder the latter approach has resulted in a culture of material profusion, whereas the former approach has nurtured a culture of spiritual resplendence.

The experience at the temple today was most rewarding and illuminating. In his demeanor and tone of voice, Dr. Mohan in every regard resembled a religious man. The hushed measured tones with which he described to me the history and significance of the structure, communicated a sense of the sacred. The quickening of his breath as he related the stories depicted in the carvings and murals, indicated a deep overriding attitude of reverence which was not in the least diminished by his repeated assurance, "Of course, I do not believe in these gods or these stories." He said that in spite of their non-affiliation to this or any religion, his wife and he frequently come to the temple simply for the fresh air, spaciousness and sense of peace it exudes.

From my experience these are the very qualities that characterize the Indian psyche—a general yet profound sense of reverence, a kind of detachment or spaciousness that always makes room for others and never feels cramped even in a pushing crowd, plus an appreciation of and aspiration for inner peace. I find these characteristics cut through society more than most Indians themselves even realize, linking Christians, Moslems, Hindus, and even atheists. These qualities are true to the spirit of any religion.

Specific elaborations of religious forms, rituals, imageries, stories and doctrines are primarily celebrations of the prolific human imagination rather than depictions of any external God or Truth. All spirituality is concerned with "inspiration" (literally an arousing of the spirit within). The items which inspire can be endless. Most striking is that the crucial ingredient in inspiration seems to lie within the perceiver rather than residing as an inherent quality of the perceived object. In fact, all so-called spiritual disciplines seem at least partially aimed at awakening within us the quality of perception which allows us to be inspired by an ever-widening circle of items of awareness.

Ultimately the source of inspiration resides within the very spirit that is awakened. It is as if all inspiration is a case of the spirit seeing itself reflected in outward forms and feeling itself liberated from its imagined status as an "imprisoned splendor" within the body boundaries, circumlimited by time and space.

Thus the essence of what I prefer to think of as spirituality rather than "religiousity" is quite common and evident as a thread running through the collective psyche of India. Appropriately enough, it took the reverence of an atheist to drive this fact home to me.

As I write these words, I am feeling the excitement of being on the eve of a homecoming. Our next destination is Varkala. There, we will spend two weeks in the gurukula I stumbled into fifteen years ago. That stumbling proved to be a turning point in which irritation became inspiration, a pleasure cruise became a pilgrimage, an aversion to philosophy became a thirst for wisdom, and a troubled heart revealed itself to be an ocean of peace.

24

The Land Of Prince

Notes from a bamboo flute splatter like raindrops and cry like a forlorn love bird, weaving a magic spell. Sixteen of us are resting in the middle of a rare outing from the gurukula with Guru. It is rare both in the sense of "precious" and in the sense of "unusual."

During the past five days those of us participating in the current East West University semester have been staying at Varkala, the headquarters of both the Narayana Gurukula and the East West University itself. Guru has been conducting three classes a day plus working-in some additional English dictations to me in the early mornings.

In class Guru has been speaking about the nature of the self. According to Indian thought, at its base the self is Existence, Consciousness, and Bliss. This is similar to the self-declaration of God in the Bible as "I am that I am." Wherever there is an "I am," there is existence and awareness. The awareness of existence or existence of awareness is the most cherished absolute value of which all relative values are but fragmentary reflections. Simply to know we exist unconditionally or simply to exist as pure knowledge, without any extraneous qualifications, is blissful.

Then how is it that this is not our normal experience?

Through the process of veiling, projection and partiality, that vast "I am" becomes limited as "I am this" or "I am that," and the pure formless consciousness modulates into temporary specific forms. As a result, the affectivity of the originally blissful self is experienced as a spectrum ranging from agony to ecstasy. Thus mistaken identity or ignorance of the real self is at the very heart of all the desires and fears, comedies and tragedies that constitute our life drama.

In reality it is only our perception of the self that undergoes transformation and not the self itself. The self remains as a constant, an eternal presence, below all the surface agitations, as a self-aware existence. Spiritual discipline partially consists of a process of self-recollection whereby one disengages one's identity from the surface modifications of one's mind and reestablishes oneself in one's imperturbable core. When such an identity is established, one recognizes the very same "I am" at the heart of all beings. From this perspective, compassion becomes natural or simply, as Jesus described, "loving one's neighbor *as one's self.*"

(Before leaving India I was to see this time-honored Indian "theory" that bliss is the underlying nature of the self put to a severe test.)

As a refreshing break from the intensive classes, we are today visiting the enchanted "Land of Prince." Prince, as I mentioned earlier, is the name of one of Guru's young Malayalee students. He is proudly guiding us on a tour of his village environs. First we were shuttled by hired cars to a lagoon at the confluence of several backwater canals. After a short walk past palms, mango trees, jackfruit trees and numerous unidentified greeneries, we all loaded into a large wooden outrigger canoe. As most of the Malayalees do not know how to swim, the adventure was not without the thrill of faint fear.

Smoothly, slowly, silently we glided out to the middle of the lagoon, powered by manual labor and one single long bamboo pole pushed against the shallow bottom. The silence was periodically pierced with shouted jokes and laughter, some of it of the nervous variety. The chatter and jokes were in Malayalam, which left my mind free to drink in the gentle silent manner our craft cut through the water.

In all directions, for 360 degrees along the lagoon's shores, were groves and hillsides awash in the frilly green of coconut palms. I would not have believed that in a single sweep of the head one could take in so many of this magnificent form of life. The coconut palm has come to symbolize for me the hospitality and abundance of Nature, as well as the ingenuity and generosity of my own species. The feeling coconut palms generate in me must be akin to the feeling most Indians experience at a temple or before the image of one of their 33 million gods.

Our destination, as if we needed one, was a lush green island smack dab in the middle of the lagoon upon which sat a small unmanned temple at the foot of a huge banyan tree. Upon arriving, Guru seated himself beside the tree, closed his eyes and without notice began dictating the next Malayalam verse and commentary. As if from nowhere some paper appeared, and soon most of the Malayalees were busily scribbling at Guru's feet.

Penelope, a long-time American friend and associate, here with her son and daughter, commented "I don't understand it. When an American sees a body of water like this, all we can think of is diving in. But when a Malayalee sees it, they just want to look at it briefly and move on."

I suggested, "It must be like whenever and wherever they see a temple, they are compelled to dive in, whereas we just look and pass on." She laughed, and without any further ado, we slipped back down to the shore and into the brackish water.

Floating on my back with the sun caressingly warm on my face, I thought "So this is The Land of Prince." Indeed I had fallen into a fairyland. Just then, Prince himself floated by in the canoe with two baskets of tender coconuts and a long bunch of ripe bananas still on the stem. Several of the Indians had joined Penelope, Aruna (her daughter), and me in the water. They too were obviously caught up in the fairy tale or otherworldly atmosphere. They pleaded with Prince to toss them the fruit right there, where they stood, for the pure indulgence of partaking while standing or floating in the sensual water.

I shouted to Prince how much I was relishing this day in

his princedom. He called back that this was only a small portion of "The Land of Prince," and soon we would all be going to his "castle," which was right on the Arabian Sea where we could have another swim.

At that moment I had the idea for a children's story called "The Land of Prince." The prince grows up on this very island, loving the area and being very proud the island is his. Because he loves The Land of Prince so much, he never wants to leave. Slowly he begins to explore and discovers more and more of the adjacent area is also a continuation of the same Land of Prince. Ultimately, he discovers that however far he roams, the mutual embrace of his own loving nature and the boundless world without make the entire world The Land of Prince.

The general euphoria included a tinge of sadness on the return canoe ride. The only regret was that my camera was in Trivandrum for repairs and I would not be able to share with friends the visual images of this fairyland. In particular a fantastic photo I could take only in my mind's eye was of Guru and Jyoti snuggled up to each other in the middle of the boat. Jyoti was wearing a floppy blue sailor's hat pulled down almost to her sunglasses, and Guru was holding his walking stick and sporting a white towel wrapped around his head and tied under his chin, easter-bonnet style. The two of them were framed by the blue of sky and green of palms.

The awaiting cars drove us the short distance to the beach and Prince's family. There we were serenaded by the flute recital of Prince's father, with which I commenced this tale. The music was followed by a delicious multi-dish meal, a short nap, some body-surfing in the Arabian Sea, Guru's English translation of his morning dictation, several tender coconut juices and a big red banana. Only after all this did we return to the more earthly paradise of Varkala.

25

In The Garden Of Faith

Varkala is a thriving coastal village thirty miles north of Trivandrum, the Kerala State capital. The narrow roadways are rich with the fragrance of jasmine and plumeria blossoms. The people are primarily fisherfolk, merchants, farmers, and craftspeople. They are generally poor in terms of money but lavishly provided with coconuts (Kerala means "The Land of the Coconut"), forty-seven varieties of bananas, fertile rice fields, cashews, and some pretty exotic but nourishing fruits and vegetables with such names as jackfruit, breadfruit, elephant yam, and drumsticks.

It is not a widely known fact, but according to the latest World Health Organization's figures, India has recently become statistically "self-sufficient" in the production of wheat and rice. In other words, each year there is now enough wheat and rice produced within the country as a whole to feed every man, woman, and child in India. Unfortunately there are dire political problems that are preventing equitable distribution. It is the greed, hoarding, and injustice of many politicians and landowners which are behind the problem of hunger in India and not any inadequacy of Nature's abundance.

Almost every family in Varkala has at least one cow, which instead of slaughtering for food, they worship. The economic blessing behind this religious posture is that, in prolonging the health of the cow, the people are in turn provided daily with milk, butter and yogurt long after the single season in which the meat would be consumed and done with. These marvelous sacred cows, in being left to their own devices, also serve as twin-bellied street cleaners and producers of "pies" used for fertilizer, cooking fuel, and (believe it or not) floor surfacing. In ambling across roads at their slightest whim and often even selecting the center of the road as an ideal site for a siesta, the cows often function as organic traffic controllers. Our traffic police could only be envious at the reverence these four-legged "cowps" receive.

The gurukula itself has a beautiful gate with a wrought iron rising sun, through which one enters a sandy courtyard shaded by mango and hibiscus trees and surrounded by a circle of whitewashed, red-roofed buildings. The largest building is a dining room and kitchen complex where meals are prepared on wood, coconut husk, and palm frond fires. Recently a methane burner has been added which is fueled by the biomass produced by the gurukula cows. Thus the gurukula has moved directly from the pre-industrial age to the post-industrial "new age," without the interim industrial phase of using either electricity or fossil fuels for cooking food.

Other buildings include an office with a small living quarters upstairs, two large dormitories, several compact two person huts, a library, a bath house, and a row of latrines. There are two deep wells, and since my first visit a pump has been added to one of them, providing periodic running water. In addition to the mango trees, there are coconut palms, papaya trees, and a jackfruit tree. Behind the living quarters there is a vegetable garden and a large soccer field on the other side of which is the two-storied press where spiritual books are typeset and printed manually by a cheerful group of young men and women who live in the locality.

Approximately twenty-five young boys, aged 6-12, are boarding here and attending the public school across the street. At the gurukula, in addition to being helped with their regular school subjects, they are taught the precepts of the spiritual traditions of all the world's major religions.

I enjoy watching them during these morning and evening sessions, sometimes absorbed in chanting or listening to Guru's lessons (presented in Malayalam, with capsule English translations) and at other times letting their minds wander freely on invisible wings. This daydreaming is what I remember most from my own religious training. But these lessons obviously carry importance for these boys, and they only infrequently appear restless.

Today a man came and took Guru, Jyoti and myself to his house for lunch. The taxi drove us to a small remote village and then pulled off the paved road and onto a deeply rutted dirt road. The clay soil seemed an almost impossibly luminescent red.

As we wound through the tropical jungle, houses peeked out at us. Half-hidden in all the greenery, huts of mud and thatch sat as next door neighbors to lavish brick and plaster houses. These fancy homes are products of the "Gulf Boom," whereby for about ten years Keralans flocked by the tens of thousands as literate, semi-skilled and relatively cheap labor for the tentatively mushrooming Arab oil economy. The boom has now inevitably gone bust for the Malayalees, due both to plummeting oil prices on the world market and to the Arabs' discovery of still cheaper sources of labor elsewhere in Asia and the Philippines. Anyway, these patchwork multi-class neighborhoods are part of the petro-fallout. The children from all the houses were indistinguishable, as they stopped their games at the unusual sound of a car coming down their road and gaped in awe as the swami and the whiteman rode by smiling.

Along the way we stopped at the top of a rise and ourselves gaped in awe at the spectacular view of a palm-lined lake lying below. The scene was made more, not less, alluring by the houses that speckled the shore. The evidence of human habitation transformed the implication of wilderness into the even higher order of "Garden of Eden." Guru agreed when I speculated Kerala either had been in fact the Garden of Eden, or else it had inspired the legend.

We got out of the taxi where the road narrowed, rendering vehicular traffic impossible, and strolled the last quarter mile to our host's home. His family of eight were, and must have been for generations, living in a basic one-room hut with a thatched roof and woven palm frond siding. With the proceeds from a recently published children's book on Narayana Guru, he was constructing a small four-room brick house.

Out of the tiny hut came a meal surpassing the high-tech kitchens of four-star hotels in New York City. It consisted of the usual rice, curries, yogurt and condiments, but by any standard it would qualify as gourmet.

The tongue relishes this Indian food as much as the eyes relish a panoramic sunset. In fact, all the five senses participate integrally in the appreciation of each Indian meal. The eyes are dazzled by the colors, such as the orange of tumeric, the red of chilies, and the yellow of saffron. Similarly is the nose delighted by the extravagance of spices. Nor does the sensuality of an Indian meal end there. Eating with one's fingers, turns a meal into an extraordinarily tactile experience as well. Finally, one learns to appreciate even the subtle distinctive sounds of preparation, such as of coconut being shredded and mustard seeds popping in hot oil.

As we sat outside the hut waiting for lunch, I was dazzled by the abundance of banana, coconut, mango, jackfruit and cashew trees sprinkled liberally throughout the neighborhood. The absence of roads or even compound walls guarantees that the fruit of these trees is common property. I think by prevailing Western criteria for "standard of living," the Garden of Eden itself would have been condemned as an underdeveloped pocket of poverty.

At our feet scurried a mother hen and about a dozen little chicks, all pecking here and there on the ground, the mother more vigorously than the rest. Guru pointed out to me how the mother herself was not actually eating at all but rather, with each peck, was pointing out the exact location of a grain or seed or whatever, which one of the chicks would then pick up and eat. I marveled at this selfless demonstration of loving care which Nature, the mother of all, has planted instinctively in the hen. Evidently no cogitation or calculation whatsoever is necessary for the hen to carry out Nature's generous program. Once again I was reminded of the faith-instilling words of Jesus:

> Look at the birds in the sky. They neither reap nor sow nor store away in barns, and yet your heavenly Father [read: *Nature*, if you prefer] feeds them... And why worry about clothes? Consider the lilies of the field. They neither work nor weave, but I tell you that even King Solomon in all his glory was never arrayed like one of these. Now if God so clothes the flowers of the field, which are alive today and burned tomorrow, is He not much more likely to clothe you, oh ye of little faith?

With respect to Christ's vision presented here and having lived below, at, or near the so-called "poverty line" for decades, Nataraja Guru once asked his disciple, Nitya, "What is the most valuable possession a person can have?" Smelling a trick, Nitya refrained from speculating, but eagerly asked, "What is it, Guru?" To which Guru replied, "A torn shirt. For nothing could take him or her down to the market faster to get a new one." I will have opportunity to comment further on this "economics of abundance" as it contrasts with our "economics of scarcity." Certainly Jesus and Nataraja Guru had unshaken faith in the former.

Just this morning Guru had been speaking in class of "God" as the inner controlling principle. From the time of the union of the sperm and egg into a single cell, something has meticulously manufactured this uncanny complex organism of ours with its miraculous powers of perception, cogitation and action. That same wise and skillful principle continues to function within us, masterfully carrying out countless operations such as the circulation of our blood, the regulation of our body temperature, the digestion of our food, its conversion into both energy and building blocks, the maintenance of memory and the recall of just the appropriate associations called for by each freshly presented gestalt. These are but a few of the mysterious and ingenious workings of our inner nature.

Our inner nature and nature outside are blended in such a way that one cannot but sense an overriding factor fashioning our many worlds. It is the realization and glorification of this dynamic which is at once the source and goal of all religions, be they theistic or atheistic.

With a full belly from our "humble" feast and a satisfied mind, I bounced along in the taxi as we retraced the red-rutted road back to the gurukula. This was the eve of the annual gurukula convention. Each year at this time, the simple uncrowded and peaceful atmosphere of the gurukula is transformed into a noisy surging ocean of merry-making well-wishers. I had already experienced the hurly-burly of several of these affairs and had decided this year I would stay as far away from the action as possible, perhaps hanging out at the gorgeous beach in Varkala for the interim.

As if reading my mind (which wouldn't have been the first time), Guru turned to me and asked if I had read the convention program yet. When I answered, "No," he suggested that I take a look at it when we get back. There was a mischievous glint in his eye which I found a bit unsettling.

26

Inaugural Address

Surprise! Upon returning to the gurukula, I walked into the office and asked to see a copy of the convention program. Sure enough near the top, amidst the indecipherable Malayalam squiggles was my name. I had to ask somebody to translate it. Evidently I was slated to deliver the Inaugural Address the next morning to open the six day convention. Swallowing a lump of irritation at not having been informed (not to mention "asked"), I resolved to take it as an honor and a challenge.

To prepare myself I sought the solitude of a nearby hilltop and pondered what I might like to say. I decided from the very beginning that I wouldn't side-step the irony of paying tribute to the gurukula's peaceful contemplative environment within the circus atmosphere generated during the week of the convention. I wanted to offer an alternative that would honor our intent in congregating for this occasion.

The notion of "congregating" proved to be the thread I followed late into the night and again from early in the morning to develop my theme. Every spiritual tradition prizes the role of the congregation. None does so more specifically than Buddhism which proclaims the congregation to be one of the "Three Refuges." Although many associate the gurukula movement with Hinduism, it is intended to embrace truth and beauty in all their expressions. Thus I considered it appropriate to wrap my reflections in a Buddhist framework.

The next morning several hundred people were gathered at the gurukula for the opening ceremony. Guru was presiding. When the time came for the Inaugural Address, he skipped over it and began introducing the next speaker. My heart skipped a beat and I became flushed with mixed emotions. "All that work for nothing," I thought.

One of his older students pointed out I was to present the Inaugural Address. Guru sort of waved him away and said, "Never mind. He doesn't like to make public speeches." I didn't know whether he was having some fun with me, trying to teach me some lesson, or simply trying to protect me. It is true I usually try to bow out of public speaking when possible.

I tried to console myself with the thought, "At least the process of preparation has been meaningful to me."

The other student persisted on my behalf, "But Guru, Peter has prepared something."

"Oh alright," he said, "have him come up here."

After all that I was too befuddled to be nervous. Guru gave me a nice introduction, and then I presented the address I had prepared. This is the gist of what I said:

"The three most important factors in the spiritual life of a Buddhist are the *Buddha*, the *Dharma*, and the *Sangha*. These they call their 'three refuges.' These factors can be understood in such a way as to have great relevance in the life of any person regardless of our spiritual or philosophical orientation. One need not be a Buddhist to be elevated by their implications.

How are these three 'refuges' to be understood?

"The dharma literally means 'the law'. It is this inner law which determines both the structure and function of each atom, cell, and organ in our bodies, as in all animate and inanimate matter. It is this law, operating as *swadharma* (one's own foundation), that determines and constitutes the unique personality of each of us as well as the particular 'calling' or meaning which constitutes each's personal fulfillment. Thus we can take refuge, find consolation and inspiration in the dharma, or lawfulness that makes each thing what it is and harmoniously related to all other things.

"Buddha, literally the Awakened One, represents the Light of Consciousness, which is at once a vision of Truth or Eternal Reality and at the same time the Truth or Reality thus envisioned. Consciousness is both subject and object of such a vision. We can take refuge in this bright substratum, eternally at the core of our own being. In theistic religions this omnipresent and immortal Light of Consciousness is referred to as the Godhead.

"If the dharma can be said to bubble up like an underground spring or rise up from our roots like a sprout from a seed, the buddha can be seen to descend like a shower of grace or the rays of the sun, warming and nourishing all life below. Again, to be meaningful these factors are to be recognized as inner dynamics operating within our own selves as well as everywhere in the world around us. In fact, there is no inner and outer with regard to either this law or this light.

"But the law itself is not a manifest thing, nor in the light of pure consciousness is there any*thing* to be seen. It is only in the sangha (the congregation) that these two factors meet and become manifest. The congregation is the Word become flesh, so to speak. Thus we also take refuge, seek consolation, understanding and inspiration in the sangha. Although normally the congregation is limited to include only the followers of a certain religion, in reality our sangha consists of the congregation of all beings, or more unitively stated, 'of all being.'

"It is to experience and celebrate our membership in that congregation that we gather here for this convention. We are the Word become flesh. We are the continuation of the same song that Narayana Guru sang in his hymns. Our lives are the demonstrable elaboration of his philosophical expositions. We can be the harmoniously lawful presentation of the law. We can be the enlightened presentation of the light.

"Human beings have a freedom not found elsewhere in this created world. We are free to be sloppy, foolish and disruptive. Ostensibly we are congregating here to share and glorify the teachings of Narayana Guru and to resonate with the truth expounded by all the Great Teachers of all time and clime. Yet there are two roads before us. In our coming together, we can create a climate of essential fusion or an atmosphere of non-essential confusion.

"To be frank, my experience of four previous gurukula conventions has been that they tend more toward confusion than fusion. For fifty-one weeks out of any year, I find Varkala to be one of the most peaceful spots on earth, almost irresistibly conducive to a clear contemplative frame of mind. For the other one week each year, the week of the convention, the Varkala gurukula turns into a noisy chaotic bazaar-type atmosphere, filled with the disturbing distractions of a crowd drowning in gossip and small-talk.

"Narayana Guru himself, in whose name we gather this week, gives us a strikingly clear understanding of the nature of "small-talk" and its impact on the contemplative or spiritual life. The following is an English translation of his 'Nivritti Panchakam (Five Verses on Inward Release).'

What name? Caste? Trade? How old?
From questions such when one is free,
One gains release.

Come! Go! Go not! Enter! What seekest?
From utterances such, when one is free,
One gains release.

Departest when? When arrived? Whence and even who?
From questions such, when one is free,
One gains release.

I or thou; this and that; inside or out; or none at all;
From cogitations such, when one is free,
One gains release.

To the known and the unknown equalized;
differenceless to one's own or that of others;
even to the name of such, indifferent;
From all considerations such, one freed,
Oneself, becomes the one released.

"If we are to take seriously the words of the guru here and refrain from indulging in discussion of the above-censored topics, most likely we will, at least initially, be left in silence. It is that very silence in which Narayana Guru spent his fondest hours and from which he mined the gems of wisdom which we so treasure today.

"In silence we reach the place from whence all things originate. It is in silence that we come face to face with our true Self. In silence we merge with unconditioned and eternal beingness. In silence the self-luminosity of consciousness shines upon itself alone. In silence the imperturbable bliss of the unbroken consciousness of pure being is known—known not as an object is known, but known as the core of the knowing subject. It is this one subjective consciousness which refracts and reflects into seemingly separate objects whenever its inherent silence is broken.

"Thus I am recommending that, as we go about our lives and programs this coming week, we make a special effort to cultivate, taste and share this rich silence. I have found again and again in many settings that, whereas the silence of one person is restfully peaceful, the cumulative silence of a number of people generates a peace of an altogether different order. Such collective silence actually emanates a positive presence and is not simply an absence of sound as one might expect.

"Let the words we speak emanate from and in some way be expressive of silence. Let us only break the silence reluctantly and with the intention to improve upon it, if such be possible. Jesus said, 'Man does not live by what goes into the mouth, but rather by every word that issueth forth from the mouth of God.' God has no other mouths with which to speak than ours. Let us take up this role consciously and responsibly and speak only those words which we would be proud to attribute to God. Let the wondrous law (dharma), which creates and regulates all life, and the mysterious self-conscious light (buddha), which illuminates all creation, be embodied in and as our congregation (sangha)."

After I sat back down, Guru took the microphone and in Malayalam presented a brief synopsis of my address. Although he gave me no direct indication of what he had thought of my presentation, I learned from a Malayalee friend that Guru had announced his wish to incorporate an aspect of my thesis into the daily program of the convention. Guru requested that each morning, from the time the bell signalled breakfast until the day's first seminar session ninety minutes later, there be a collective observation of silence.

As I walked back up to our hilltop hut, I had the light-headed feeling of accomplishment and relief that used to accompany the completion of a final exam in college.

27

The Presence And Presents Of The Guru

Well, we all survived the convention. In fact, it went very smoothly. Even including the festive evening performances of classical and folk music and dance, which were of a very high quality, there was indeed an underlying current of peace and quietude among the several hundred congregated for the convention. I do not attribute this to the influence of my inaugurating suggestion so much as I see that my address may have emanated from and given expression to a collective intention that most likely was prevailing synchronistically in many of us at once.

The day after my presentation a friend brought me a copy of the local newspaper featuring a most unflattering photograph of me delivering my address. The snapshot caught me with a queasy expression, looking as though I am choking down some sour medicine for a bad case of constipation. My forty cent Varkala haircut is so short, my hair looks like it is painted on. Worst of all, Guru appears to be enjoying a good snooze sitting at my side.

In a most fitting epilogue, three days later Aruna rushed up to me full of excitement. She had been shopping down at the vegetable market, and the shopkeeper had wrapped her cauliflower up in a scrap of newspaper with my photograph on it. Not exactly a bid for immortality but at least something to write home to mom about.

I felt honored, paradoxically to the point of humility, that Guru invited me to share his small room with him during our two weeks in Varkala. In spite of the ebb and flow of a continuous crowd of people to receive his blessing and the nearly ceaseless flood of Malayalam, I feel tremendously regenerated as a result of his constant presence.

He somehow gave each person the impression that they were the most important person in the world to him, which for those moments indeed they were. I marveled at the patience with which he gave his full attention to each one's problems, prides, dreams and questions. Sometimes I watched, or even I myself escaped, as in spite of exhaustion, hunger or a longing to bathe, Guru would sit and listen to an entire book of an old man's unpublished poems, a lengthy journal chronicling another man's marital problems, or the long-winded rantings of an obviously unstable woman.

With wisdom, compassion and humor, he would respond spontaneously and uniquely to each one, who would then leave with gratitude and a renewed sense of direction and self-worth written on their features. Sometimes after all had gone and the lights were finally out, he would speak to me in the darkness from under his mosquito net and translate the highlights of several of the day's encounters.

I see each person's relationship with Guru as a staff with which they can mount the mountain or molehill of their problems and see from above, as it were, more clearly. A tiny bubble bursting on the froth of a fragment of a small wavelet rising on a river, when viewed from the sea seems most insignificant, but when viewed from within that bubble itself, it must necessarily seem catastrophic.

Guru's radical economic theories have been put into practice this week. Whatever he received with one hand (an amazing flow of money, fruit and prepared delicacies) was immediately distributed from the other hand to others who came. Nothing was held back for himself, although as his big belly (which today he referred to as his "jellyfish") attests, he would sample each snack. This uncommon and extremely promising approach to personal and collective economics has an essential commonality with the "Hippie Economics" practiced during the late 1960's in San Francisco.

The theory behind Hippie Economics was best explained by Jerry Garcia, musician and counterculture guru, who described the overcrowded but thriving scene of dropouts and flower children living in the Haight Ashbury district during its heyday. In effect what he said was, "The scene was composed of very many people and very little money. What we discovered was that if you take that little bit of money and keep it moving around very fast, it becomes as if there is actually a great deal of money in circulation. Hence both the receiving and spending powers of all individuals within that community are greatly enhanced."

The main difference between the hippie version and Guru's version of the same principle is that the former was based on an assumption of scarcity whereas the latter assumes a natural state of abundance as its starting point. This very well reflects a fundamental difference in the two cultures in which each approach has its roots. Thus for Robin Hood to function in the West, he must necessarily steal from the rich (who are hoarding against the fear of scarcity) in order to give to the poor; whereas for Guru to manage his heartwarming redistribution, he only has to receive of the outpouring of gifts freely given (in recognition and appreciation of a mysterious abundance) by the people of India.

One time during my second or third trip to India, Guru and I were waiting on a platform as our train steamed into the station. Just as I was gathering up both of our luggage, a coolie scampered up to me and motioned that he would carry our things on board. Partially out of a pride of self-sufficiency and partially out of my habitual "frugality," I waved him away. Guru took me aside and sternly asked me, "Have you had your breakfast this morning?"

"Yes," I answered. He knew very well I'd had my breakfast, because I had been sitting next to him when I did.

"Well then, how can you begrudge this man the opportunity to earn his?"

Guru pictures the flow of money as being like water through a pipe. If the tap is closed down restraining the outflow, then no new water will flow in and through the pipe. Conversely, so long as water is flowing out, fresh water will continuously flow in.

Once in Portland when I was trying to save him a few bucks by "comparison shopping" for a typewriter he needed to purchase, he stopped me with the explanation, "I have an economic consideration most people don't have. If I don't spend this money this week in Portland, then the money that may be coming to me next week in San Francisco won't come." As far as I am able to tell, the consistent practice of this radical economics has never left him seriously wanting. This extends to the giving of his time and energy in the same manner as of his rupees and dollars.

The most powerful method of teaching is not through pontification, but through modeling in one's own behavior the verity and value of what is being taught. In many ways the rebellion of the sixties was a sometimes violent reaction to the "Do as I say and not as I do" approach to instruction on the part the previous generation. With regard to modeling, Guru is indeed a teacher *par excellence*.

Last night we came to Radha's house. She is a longtime student and devotee of Guru. I slept well until 3:30AM when the power went off and with it the ceiling fan which had been rendering mosquito aerial raids impossible. The next two hours were spent applying and reapplying lemon grass oil and squirming to keep myself covered by a sheet which provided the choice of too hot or too exposed to attack.

This morning I gazed appreciatively out of Radha's front door across a mere ten feet of swept sand courtyard beyond which dense lush jungle was licking at the fringes. In addition to the ever-present coconut palm, I could make out shiny-leafed banana trees, lace-like "flame of the forest" trees, climbing vines and creepers and numerous wild flowering bushes, all thriving on the carbon dioxide we exhale and converting it back into the oxygen which constitutes our life's breath. The literal meaning of *conspiracy* is "breathing together." This then, is a true conspiracy of Nature. Even the mosquitoes are co-conspirators!

28

The Extended Self & Its Intended "Other"

The midday Indian sun turns her train cars into baking hot ovens. Even in the relative comfort of first class, where 25% of the fans work as opposed to 5% in second class, I feel like an overdone pastry. Perhaps the most unforgettable photographs of my 1980 trip to India with Carolyn and the kids (Aaron and Rachel, then 8 and 10) were individual portraits of each of the three of them, smiling gamely but looking wrung out of vitality and limply hung out to dry at the fag end of an all day train ride down Kerala's Malabar Coast.

This time I am making the run solo. I left Guru and company in Calicut. They are heading northeast into the foothills of the Wynad Mountains for a week of classes at the lakeside Vythiri Gurukula. I am heading south to Cochin to meet my friend Drow from California. Drow is flying down from a trek in Nepal for a brief one week visit to India.

When I learned of Drow's plans in November, just as I was preparing to leave, I offered to meet him and play tour-guide. Since then, as the idea has grown on me, I have made arrangements to pick him up at the airport and whisk him to the house of one of my favorite families in India. At that house the home-cooking is as delicious as the family is friendly as the house is comfortable. While in Cochin, I plan to escort Drow to see the otherworldly "psychedelic" form of classical Kerala dance known as *Kathakali*. Drow himself is a dancer. Then I hope to arrange for us to take an outrigger canoe ride along the famous and still unspoiled Kerala backwater canals.

After that I want to take him down to Varkala to see the Gurukula, the East West University Headquarters and, not least of all, the beach there, which is my favorite of all the beaches I have seen around the world so far. While in Varkala, I have arranged with Prince and his friend, Sree Kumar, to pick us up at the Gurukula on their motor scooters and ride us back for a return trip to the now fabled "Land of Prince."

I find I have a foreboding hunch that Drow will not be meeting me as planned. Perhaps this all sounds to me "too good to be true." During the past two months of no contact, Drow may have changed his plans, or perhaps I don't trust Indian Airlines' ability to honor their reservations, or maybe I have an intuition of some other unknown interference. We'll see tomorrow.

We were in Calicut for five days staying at the home of a wealthy, generous and intriguing family. Their several problems and squabbles could easily be the subject of a fascinating soap opera. Whereas Guru sat in quiet arbitration over the family's most explosive overriding riddles, I was modestly approached by a few individual family members to help them sort out some personal issues.

I was very touched by the humility, candor and trust with which the difficulties were presented. I have noticed throughout my experience counselling, both professionally and casually, that these three qualities within a seeker act as keys which somehow unlock reserves of empathy and insight within myself, which may otherwise be much more difficult for me to tap. Still, I have learned far more than I was able to offer from these recent sessions, particularly about the suffocatingly close bonds and prescribed roles of the Indian family set-up.

The rewarding reassurance that the benefit was mutual came when the same individuals who had approached me for "counselling" turned around and recommended that a divorced woman neighbor and a married couple in crisis also sit and talk with me about their situations. There was a common strangulating thread in all of these several scenarios. Societal expectations, pressures and outright meddling time and again were thwarting the good intentions and drive toward creative self-expression of the troubled persons. The very individuals who were the victims of society's hang-ups would then wind up seriously questioning their own self-worth, inner imperatives and general sanity. I have neither seen nor heard of any society which does not have this crippling side-effect on at least some of its members.

In addition to Guru's ongoing daily morning classes on "Experiential Aesthetics and Imperiential Transcendence," he had two major public evening talks. The theme of the evening presentations was "*tat tvam asi*," which is one of the four great Sanskrit dictums of the *Upanishads*. The translation of this dictum is "That thou art."

The story or context is of a young man, named Svetaketu, who at the age of twenty-four returns to his family home after his long years of schooling, all puffed up with pride. He even tells his father to ask him anything, and he will be able to answer.

Shocked at this arrogance, his father asks him, "OK, please tell me what is that which once it is known everything becomes known and not knowing which nothing is truly known?" Now it was the son's turn to be shocked. Svetaketu said, "I do not know any such thing. My teachers also must not have known this. If you know it, then please accept me as your student and teach it to me."

The father then proceeds to illustrate the nature of the essential self in all beings through seven beautiful and thought-provoking illustrations (see *Chandogya Upanishad* in Robert Hume's *Thirteen Principle Upanishads*). The Universal Self is compared to the salt that evenly pervades the ocean—yielding the same essential flavor throughout, to a tiny fig seed in which an entire fig tree is lying hidden, and to the one water that assumes various identities such as vapor, cloud, rain, river, and ocean, etc.

At the conclusion of each illustration, the father proclaims,

"That thou art, Svetaketu." Ultimately the entire world of the known as well as that which remains unknown is to be seen as of the finest essence of the seer's own self. Thus "*tat tvam asi*" becomes a dictum of instruction for meditation and realization.

Here again the student of Indian wisdom is led away from the habitual perspective of seeing oneself in the world to the more expansive vision of seeing the world in one's self. It is said that just as it is impossible for a wave to escape the ocean, for wherever it goes the ocean is by definition there with it, similarly it is impossible for our experience to be of anything other than our own consciousness.

One practical effect of such a vision of the self is that it converts the contracted feeling of loneliness into the expansive experience of aloneness. In this sense, loneliness implies a projection of some "other(s)" and then further posits an exclusion of oneself from the other selves. If we break down the word "alone," on the other hand, to see its derivation, it reveals itself to be an abbreviated form of "all one" and thus refers to the highest state of all-inclusive union in which nothing remains outside. In aloneness there is no other to which to relate or from which to feel estranged.

If one reflects upon one's experience, one will find the absence of peace is always characterized by the agitation of desire and/or fear. Where there is no fear and no desire, there is peace. Yet both fear and desire presuppose some "other." Desire implies some sense of deficiency and some sense of something other to be attained. Similarly, all fear is of something or someone other that poses a threat. Hence where there is no "other," there is no desire and no fear, and therefore peace.

The very notion that there is a single Absolute Self, co-extensive with each of us, has become alien to the Western mind. Yet this vision forms the very atmosphere in which the Indian psyche lives and breaths. Ironically the notion of the unbroken unity of all being is entering the Western psyche through the backdoor, as it were, given the latest findings in such fields as quantum mechanics and subatomic physics.

The first night Guru explained the philosophical import of "*tat tvam asi*," and the second night he presented its implications and applications for ethics and social development. All of us found the two nights stirring and elevating. It is my intention to put together a more thorough report of the talks elsewhere.

Another highlight of our stay in Calicut was the instant and profound friendship, or rather "love affair," that blossomed between Mithu, a ten year old boy of our host family, and myself. The real seed or cause of these things remains forever hidden, but its flowers and fruits are very tangible.

Mithu speaks a flawless English, which makes my own brand of "American" seem quite crude by comparison. He is sweet, alert, extremely curious, and wise beyond his years. His aunt, Shyla, whom I also like very much, refers to him as a "precocious brat." So, I also accept his shadow side. We talked, joked, played and sat quietly together for hours.

A common ground of interest we discovered and exploited was sports. Yet even this manifested itself more as an effect than a cause of our bond of affection. For years I have remained totally indifferent to the game of cricket, in spite of the best efforts of several Indian and British friends to teach it to me and get me involved. With great fervor and patience, Mithu has now made it both understandable and interesting. In turn he showed a surprising interest to learn the rules and skills of baseball. He picked it up quickly and played several mock games of it with me. I was impressed by his ability and enthusiasm (and by beating me, he justified his aunt's description).

Our finer sentiments for one another were too subtle to be expressed and were thus primarily felt in silence. I would join him on a walk to the market when his mother sent him there, and he would sit by me as I took dictation from Guru. He is a voracious reader and was reading Hardy Boys books. Before leaving, I bought him a copy of *Tom Sawyer*. When he confessed to have already read it, I suggested I exchange it for *Treasure Island*. He had read that too, as he had *Gul-*

liver's Travels, Alice in Wonderland, King Arthur, Kidnapped and, at ten years old, the bookstore's entire section of Children's Classics. Finally he found a children's mystery he wanted to read, and I jokingly promised to send him a copy of *War and Peace* as soon as I could find one.

When he and his father dropped me at the train station this morning, we were all glad that I would be returning to Calicut and their house in a week to meet up with Guru again.

A final note on the Calicut stay: This five day visit has provided further support for my theory that the likelihood of communing with the moon and stars is in inverse proportion to the wealth of a family home. The house in which we stayed is both large and well-equipped. Part of the equipment is a high fence with a locking gate, bolts and latches on the inner and outer doors, and bars and shutters on the windows. Although this paraphernalia is designed and fitted to keep suspected others out, its actual daily effect is to keep the residents in. During our stay, the moon has waxed from empty to nearly half full, yet I have not seen it at all.

Since living for two months in a cave on Crete seventeen years ago, I have become very attached to seeing and tuning myself to the moon's phases. The poet, Robert Frost, wrote about how you think the fence you build around your house keeps your neighbor out, but even more so it keeps you fenced in. My theory is that it is not only the neighbor, but the very moon and stars, sun and clouds, which are excluded from the well-fortified and technologically well-stocked home.

The furnace-on-rails rattles on. It is becoming too hot to write. Sweaty hands make even gripping the pen problematic. The synapses of the brain are misfiring. Longing to arrive at my destination only stretches the distance to be covered. The clickety-clack seems to call out a reminder, "here and now, here and now, here and now." But my mind won't roost. It flits from thought to thought, abandoning each before it is even complete. A recurring theme is about my friend, Drow, and musings about our upcoming time together which may or may not be in the cards. Finally I sink into a heavy sleep.

29

Swept Away

What a whirlwind! My head is spinning faster than our earth. Indeed Drow did not arrive as scheduled, but showed up without warning a day later. In the five days that he was with me, constant activity, social interaction and good fun have almost eclipsed that calm "eye" which resides at rest in the heart of a hurricane.

When I learned just before leaving the U.S. that Drow would be dropping down into India for a five day first visit, I tried to imagine and arrange for him to see and experience as many of my favorite people, sights, and activities as time would allow. Now I feel I was a bit too successful. Cramming the highlights of months of my South Indian experience into a few days felt something like taking a tape of a classical piece of music, editing out the pauses and silences between notes, and playing it at a fast speed.

Drow is leaving India today, having thoroughly enjoyed much of the lush beauty of Kerala, her people and customs, but without much sense of the leisurely pace nor contemplative rhythm that underlies and overrides all the items of rich sensuality.

As usual, the state of affairs had been succinctly foreshadowed by the Chinese book of oracle wisdom, the *I Ching*. Three days before Drow's arrival, I consulted the book for guidance regarding this seven day separation from Guru and its impact on the inner development which has been initiated during this Indian stay so far. The reading

(#52) spoke of "meditation" and "inner stillness," with the following personal message:

> "You are swept along by your goals and the events you have set into motion. Even though you may wish to stop and reconsider, you cannot halt the flow of action. This condition brings unhappiness."

This bittersweet so-called "unhappiness" which was predicted, turned out not to be the unhappiness of deficiency or lack, but rather of too much pleasure to be contained. It is a sweet joy to receive, but that same reception becomes bittersweet when one's receptacle becomes full to overflowing, as if the nectar were spilling onto the floor and down the drain. Perhaps that is one of the functions of meditation: to deepen through the continual recarving of our inner vessel. Indeed in the *Bhagavad Gita* and elsewhere, the yogi is described as one into whom all the world and its varied experiences flow as do rivers into an ocean without ever causing any substantial quantitative nor qualitative change to that ocean.

What follows are the highlights of my five day trial as tour guide for a dear friend whose timetable called for a good deal more of sight-seeing than insight-seeking.

30

Dancing Gods On The Malabar Coast

On Drow's first evening in India, I escorted him to a live performance of classical South Indian dance called *Kathakali*. I had written the following about *Kathakali* dancing during my first visit to India in 1971:

"Back at the temple the famous kathakali dancing begins. Backed by four hard-driving rock congo drummers, two men playing five-foot long clarinets, two bell ringers, and two singers, the dancers with faces extravagantly painted green, red and black and with wildly colorful and ornate costumes, dance and act out stories from the Hindu scriptures with their hands and expressions. The audience (males in the center section, females off to the sides), young and old alike, is thoroughly captivated.

"Five hours later at 2:00AM they are still going strong. My energy is depleted, and I doze off. At 6:00AM I awake, and as the sun rises, the dancing is just finishing. As Prasad, at the gurukula, warned me, 'This is no mere two or three hours entertainment as you Westerners are accustomed to.' "

I cannot imagine a better verbal description and interpretation of this centuries old art form than that written by Carl Jung in his *Psychology and Religion*:

> If one carefully observes the tremendously impressive impersonations of the gods performed by the Kathakali dancers of South India, there is not a single natural gesture to be seen. Everything is bizarre, subhuman and superhuman at once. The dancers do not walk like human beings, they

glide. They do not think with their heads, but with their hands. Even their human faces vanish behind green or blue enameled masks.

The world we know offers nothing even remotely comparable to this grotesque splendor. Watching these spectacles, one is transported to a world of dreams, for that is the only place where we might conceivably meet with anything similar.

Anyone who wholeheartedly surrenders to these impressions will soon notice that these figures do not strike the Indians themselves as dream-like but as real. And indeed they touch upon something in our own depths too, with an almost terrifying intensity, though we have no words to express it. At the same time one notices that the more deeply one is stirred, the more our sense-world fades into a dream and that we seem to wake up in a world of gods, so immediate is their reality.

Even though the performance I took Drow to was an abbreviated version for tourists, we both found the dance to be very hypnotic.

The next morning we arose before dawn for a sunrise canoe ride along Kerala's famous backwater canals. Drow was putting together an audio-visual presentation of his trip, and before the sleep was even rubbed from his eyes, he was recording the symphony of bird songs which constitutes the overture to each tropical day. We caught the first bus out of town for a short ride and moderate hike to where two canoes and young paddlers awaited us.

Drow had brought the tape recorder, and the indecipherable chirpings of Malayalam gaiety blended nicely with the dawn's bird choir finale. Soon all sounds faded out, except for the "foosh" of paddle and "shoosh" of the boat cutting through the thick green water.

We passed numerous large rigs of wooden poles, pulleys, and black mesh called "Chinese nets," which would be lowered into the water and raised out almost effortlessly every few minutes to catch shrimp and small fish. Each time a net was being lifted, crows would flock above it, and before the eye could determine the existence and extent of any "catch," the crows would declare it by their own lofty indifference or feverish plunging.

Of course, coconut palms were everywhere. But here an unusual feature was that a number of them at the canal's edge had grown out horizontally over the water for a clearer dosage of sunlight. As we glided under one, I suggested to Drow, who had expressed an interest in climbing coconut trees, that he could practice on these "training palms." One family hailed us from the shore and bid us dock for some tender coconut juice, which we gladly did.

Our return trip to town took longer, as several friends of one of our guides, and some devotees of Guru's, as well as a few acquaintances of mine, wanted us to stop in at their homes. Receiving guests is considered both a blessing and an opportunity to bless, and indeed is considered a route toward accumulating karmic merit. It is very difficult and somewhat painful to decline or to rush in and out, but the alternative, especially for a sought-after Westerner, could be days and bellies both filled with tea and cookies.

The same afternoon we caught the Paresram Express for the four hour train journey down the Malabar Coast to Varkala. Our first class accommodations were roomy and comfortable, allowing me to lie down for much of the trip, which relieved my sciatic pain. The neighboring car was second class and another world—dirty, overcrowded, with hard uncomfortable benches. Back in my purer hippie days, it was a "badge of honor" to travel only second class to save both money and the shame of seeming bourgeois. I remember a couple of two and three day second class (actually *third* in those days) journeys. At the end, achy, filthy, and stinky, I felt like I was either returning from the grave or on my way in.

The train is one good way to get an overview of Indian life. The tracks run along and practically through the back yards, front yards and courtyards of Indian homes. From a window, or even better from an open doorway, you can feel the breeze, watch sunrises and sunsets over ever-changing landscapes, and witness village after village enacting their age-old daily rituals.

Pre-dawn finds men squatting in the fields performing their morning "libations and ablutions" (i.e. going to the toilet). At dawn you flash past people drawing water from wells, bathing in rivers or out of buckets and brushing their teeth with twigs. Everywhere you see people sweeping verandas and courtyards. Here and there girls and women sit in twos and threes brushing each others' long silky black hair. Soon you see the fires and smell the hot breakfasts.

Thereafter one gets to watch parades of children happily making their way to school. Many men and some women then begin toiling in the fields with at most a pair of oxen to lighten their burden. At the riversides women wash clothes by beating them against the rocks and then spread them out to dry. From a moving train on a bridge above, the drying clothes create the effect of a large colorful patchwork tapestry.

From the train door or window, the hours pass effortlessly until the blazing heat of the day transforms the villages into ghost towns. At midday the only signs of human life are the people occasionally seen sitting in the shade of trees, half asleep and half in meditation. At the first signal of the heat letting up, children seem to pop up everywhere to skip and play and shout. In the evening when the oil lamps or electric lights illuminate the interiors of the houses, families can be seen sitting for prayer, and women are seen squatting over stoves preparing the evening meal.

The most memorable incident on this particular train ride for me was a pleasant discussion initiated by two well-dressed handsome young Malayalee men. One wore a tie (the first I'd seen in weeks) and was a sales representative for a medical supply company. His name struck me as ideal for an American country and western singer, "P.B. Johnny Joseph." The other worked for a Japanese-owned chemical manufacturer.

We were speaking mostly English. I was occasionally peppering the conversation with Malayalam phrases. One of them laughed and exclaimed, "*Pinai, Malayalam manasalayo* (So then, you understand Malayalam)?"

I proudly responded, "*Adai, Malayalam pariyam* (Yes, I speak Malayalam)."

To which the other's immediate reply, full of warmth, was "Oh yes, and speak it *very* poorly." Needless to say, the remainder of our conversation was completely in English.

31

Inaction In Action

Our three days in Varkala were more of the same social and sensual enjoyment. I began to feel the need to come up for a fresh breath of contemplative peace. As all who know me will attest, I am by no means of ascetic temperament. But this was too much. We were striving to enjoy in less than a week as many activities, sights, and other items of pleasure, as in my normal rhythm in India would fill a month or two.

I've found it very helpful, especially in the flurry of movement that has characterized my life of late, to strive to follow the advice given in the *Bhagavad Gita* to "see inaction in the midst of action." There is a witnessing aspect of our self which remains unmoved by all the changing movements to which the body, emotions, mind and ego are subject. In sickness and health, pleasure and pain, certitude and doubt, humility and arrogance, this witness remains as the center in the midst of conditions, an unmoved mover, noticing change without undergoing change.

When I think of myself as a five year old, a college student, a project administrator, and now a counselor/writer, it seems like four distinct people. Yet there has been a common unbroken witnessing thread strung through all these identities, giving stability to a notion of "I" or self. This is similar to what happens in a dream. In dreams many characters, each appearing distinct from the next, can interact all within, and as aspects of, one mind.

According to the Indian world-view, we are all extensions or reflections of a single common Self, the nature of which is pure existence, pure consciousness, and pure bliss (*satchidananda*). That our existence seems temporary, consciousness limited, and bliss intermittent is attributed not to the Self but its reflecting mediums.

If you put a clear crystal on red silk, it appears to be a red crystal. The same crystal on green silk appears green. Place it before a concave or convex mirror, and the crystal will appear but in a distorted form. Surround it with smoke, and it will disappear from view.

With our own eyes we can never see our real face but only its mirror image, which is subject to all manner of colorations, distortions and opacities depending on the quality of the mirror. Our mind is like a mirror reflecting the light of the One Self. All joy or peace refers back to this unbroken, unchanging core, which is the Self of all, regardless of the specific and varied colorations conditioning its appearance. The changing variations are not the result of any action or movement of the Self, but of the mirrors or minds which by their nature belong to the plane of eternal flux and becoming.

To know this Self is to see the inaction within action. According to yoga discipline, ultimately one should keep one's mind ever restrained in the Self and see nothing but its reflection everywhere, never confusing the image with the original. I am still subject to frequent lapses during which external interests and petty inner preoccupations will dislocate me from my firm ground, resulting in temporary disequilibrium. As soon as I "come to" and realize what has happened, I can return to the center and pick up the thread again. Ideally one's meditation on the Self (the Self of all, not one's individual ego) is to be like an unbroken stream of oil continuously pouring from one vessel into another. Here, meditation is a living ever-contemplative way of life and not sitting cross-legged with one's eyes closed.

Our first afternoon in Varkala, Drow and I arrived at the beach just as the sun was setting. Magenta fingers of light fanned out from a gold-fringed cloud, turning the red-pocked cliffs into a wonderland beyond compare, although it was slightly reminiscent of the magnificent granite spires of Bryce Canyon in southern Utah.

It tickled me to think that the same sun which was just then setting into the Arabian Sea was at the very moment rising over Lake Michigan on the other side of the globe. This thought led me to the revelation that sunrises and sunsets are not periodic occurrences but constant phenomena. That is, every single moment of every day the sun is just rising over the horizon at some point on the earth. Similarly there is not one minute when the sun is not dipping into its colorful swan song somewhere else. We literally live in a world of continuous sunset and perpetual sunrise. This recognition is a case of seeing a constant (inaction) within the heart of the fleeting (action).

The waxing moon was high in the sky as night fell. Drow and I waded out into the gentle yet strong surf that provided the surfing equivalent of a "bunny hill" in skiing. With my fragile back condition, the "training waves" suited me to a "T." Drow gave me some pointers.

As the moon was playing hide-and-seek behind passing clouds, the visibility of oncoming waves in the lukewarm sea also waxed and waned. Often we had to judge the take-off required to properly catch a wave, more by sound, feel and intuition than by sight.

Suddenly the moon would burst out with a lightning-like "peekaboo" and unlike lightning linger for several seconds or even minutes. Adding magic to mystery, the inevitable signature of back-lit coconut palms cast a silhouette on the cliff tops high above us. As if to confirm that I was dreaming, the moon finished its game of hide-and-seek just as we finished our surfing, and it flood-lit our post-surf shower in the natural spring flowing out the side of one of the cliffs.

The local Malayalees who were enjoying their evening bath when we approached were very aloof and almost hostile. This understandable human reaction stems from some instinctive territoriality. Slowly and inevitably, Westerners have begun to discover the beauty and magic of this sacred beach. Over the past fifteen years I have watched the tide shift. From my being practically the only Westerner some of the locals had ever seen, there is now an influx and turnover of about a dozen or so neo-hippies at any given time. Though understandable, still I didn't appreciate being treated as the symbol of some unseen hoard. I took it as a good lesson and can now more easily see myself in visitors to our country.

According to the dialectics of yoga as revealed in the *Bhagavad Gita*, "seeing inaction within action" is only half the equation. One is also to learn to see action in inaction. It has taken me a longer time to begin to see this half of the vision.

Of course, on a surface level, the body can be inactive or sitting inert, not engaged in active pursuit of any sense objects, while at the same time the mind can be passionately engaged in ruminating on countless items of interest. This is one example of being able to recognize the action in inaction. Something still deeper is implied.

Lao Tzu in the Chinese classic, the *Tao Teh Ching*, describes how "The *tao* (Nature or simply 'The Way') never acts, yet it leaves nothing undone." This paradox touches the very core of "heaven and earth." To accomplish all without acting would seem to be impossible, and yet deep contemplation on the workings of Nature reveals just such an enigma.

A contemporary Indian sage, Sri Nisargadatta, once pointed out, "Immobility and silence are not inactive. The flower fills the space with perfume, the candle—with light. They do nothing yet they change everything by their mere presence. You can photograph the candle, but not its light. You can know a man's name and appearance, but not his influence. His very presence is action."

In some sense, being back at the Varkala Gurukula sheds a little more light on this truth. Since I was first here, this gurukula has really flowered. Several large buildings have

1. I, pictured here with a fellow student, learned that in India living creatures and natural settings are drenched in legend, myth, and spiritual significance.

2. Elephants represent Ganesha, the elephant-headed god. The large ears promote listening to wisdom. The enormous trunk aids discrimination. The small eyes minimize distraction.

3. Hanuman, the monkey hero of the epic *Ramayana*, is held up to all as a model of loyalty, agility, and unwavering purpose.

4. According to legend, a village I lived in was said to be the place where demigods, banished from heaven for fighting, were sent to earn their return by living harmoniously.

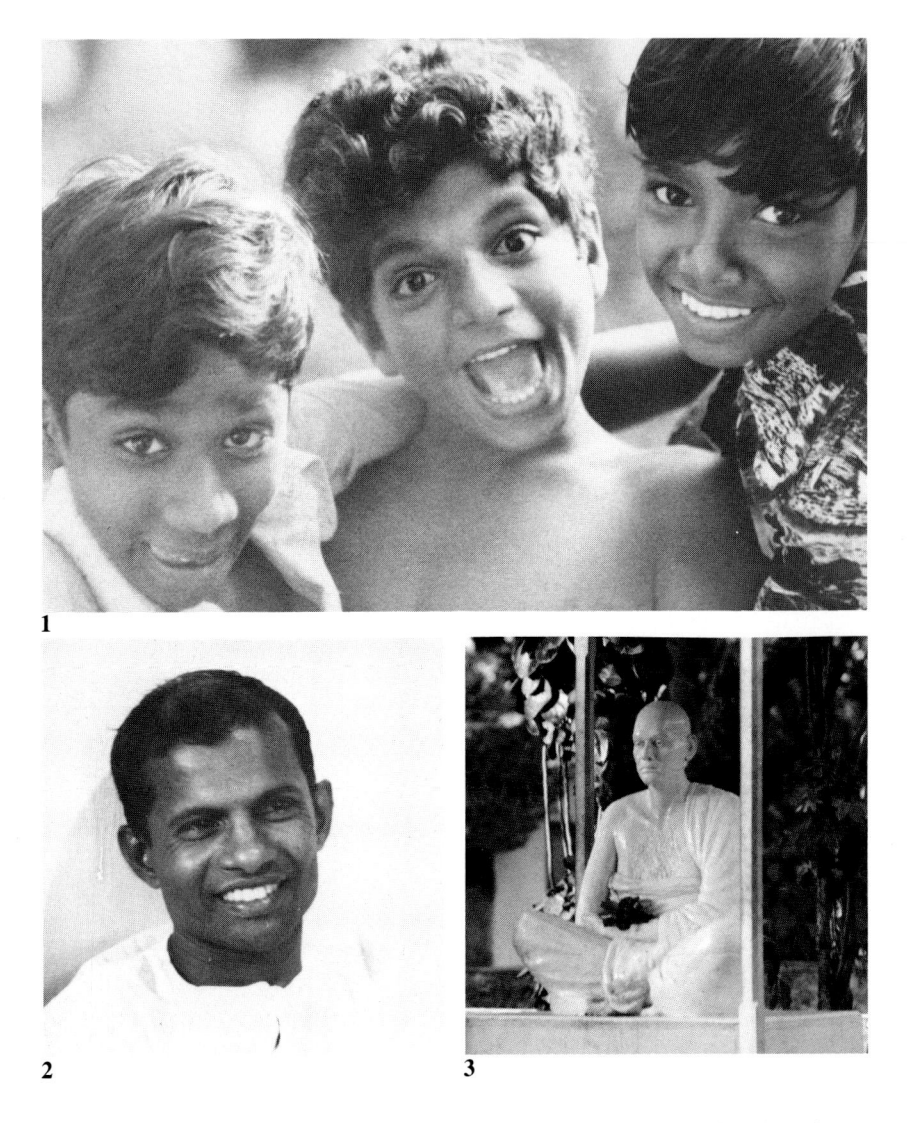

Tired of philosophy and wary of religious dogmatism, I found myself in the midst of people who attributed their joy and generosity to the life and teachings of a spiritual master.

1. In addition to the playfulness and joy characteristic of childhood, the children of the Narayana Gurukula exhibited an uncharacteristic sense of serenity and wisdom.

2. Prasad was the manager of the center into which I first stumbled by "divine mistake." He presented yoga as a science of personal peace, interpersonal harmony and creative fulfilment.

3. Statue of the spiritual master, Narayana Guru, located in the ashram.

Just as the children of India exhibit a serenity beyond their years, the elders emanate a youthful playfulness and sparkle.

1-2. Guru Nitya's ready smile and subtle humor attracted me. Through him I discovered a philosophy which provided a foundation for constant good humor.

3. Communication with Guru's non-English speaking mother was limited to expressions, gestures, and a palpable sense of her inexhaustible goodwill.

4. Anandan Swami was a man of few words and great love. His mischievous twinkle, combined with an attitude of reverence, came to symbolize for me a paradoxical constant at the heart of the Indian character.

In the West we conceive of surrender in terms of capitulation and defeat. In India surrender implies expansion beyond the confines of one's own ego into a broader self-identity. My intimate experience with the loving Anandan family demonstrated that this cultural trait may have both liberating and oppressive consequences.

1. Anandan (father), **2.** Sarojini (mother) and Tittoo (grandson), **3.** Jyoti (eldest daughter), **4.** Shanti (third daughter), **5.** Sandhya (second daughter), **6.** Baby (youngest daughter).

been added. The garden is ten times its previous size, and the boarding school has quadrupled in number of students. Growth is continuing at the same rate, but nowhere do you see the activity you would expect to accompany such radical expansion. There is some leisurely but persistent work on the gurukula buildings. Gardening demands only about a half hour per day of each resident's attention. For the most part, people seem relaxed, contented, and outwardly inactive. How is this possible?

That this aspect of Nature must remain a mystery should in no way detract from our adoration of it. Day follows night follows day, yet where is the effort in this rotation? The water of the sea is turned to vapor, raised skyward, condensed into clouds, and released again as rain. The rainwater gathers into creeks, meets other creeks forming streams, which flow together to form rivers. The rivers then carry the water necessary for life to all plants and animals. Finally all rivers empty again into the sea, and the cycle continues. Where is the effort in all this?

To paddle up a stream requires great effort. To move along with the flow requires no action at all. You can always tell when people are making use of natural forces to achieve their ends. Water doesn't worry or struggle. It simply flows along the path of least resistance, yet with all its pliability and softness, it can wear down great mountains and fill up deep valleys.

The tendencies and forces of the universe have been ordered and set in such a way that certain developments open up effortlessly one after the other. A seed becomes moist and then swells up until it bursts. Roots reach downward, and a tender sprout shoots slowly upward. The shoot hardens into a stem and eventually becomes a trunk. Branches come; leaves come; buds come, blossoming into flowers; fruits come, and at their very core develop seeds for further proliferations.

The birth, growth, transformation, reproduction, decay, and disappearance of an individual life, the life of a community, institution or entire culture are in no way separate or apart from the other natural expressions of this cosmic process. The difference is that we humans have the freedom to intelligently add to or foolishly subtract from the overall creative harmony. Anytime I am having to violently assert or force something, I can take it as a good hint I am somehow "going against the grain."

Our ongoing movement through life can be pictured as the rolling of a wheel. The farther out along the spokes of a wheel one focuses, the greater the circumference or ground covered. Yet throughout all the revolutions, the most central hub or core remains motionless. Perhaps most simply put, "action" has reference to becoming, whereas "inaction" refers to pure being. Guru once told us that if one concentrates entirely on the becoming, one becomes something of a freak; whereas if one focuses only on pure being, one becomes a big bore. The human mind can be disciplined to move freely between these two poles of movement and repose.

When I first introduced Drow to the young boys living at the Varkala Gurukula, I let slip that Drow was a good dancer. They immediately extracted a promise from him to perform a "disco" dance. After "Prayer" on our final day in Varkala, Drow made good on his promise.

The children and adults alike were stunned to see Drow's abandon and free-form spontaneity. The arts in India, particularly dance and music, are still developed within the strict guidelines and structures of classical design. I could see conflicting shadows of attraction and revulsion play across the superficially impassive faces of the observers.

For the final chorus I jumped in and joined Drow, which somehow had a kind of liberating effect on the onlookers, some of whom started clapping to the beat and hooting catcalls. Even then I noted that perplexity remained the predominant reaction in a package of mixed emotions. I once again marveled at the rich variety of cultural forms existing even in this era of the "global village" and at the spell which the relative norms and conditionings of each particular culture casts upon its members.

Later that day the two of us were sitting with Prince and his friend Sree Kumar, who had been chauffering us hither and thither on their motor scooters for three days. Prince, noticing my withdrawn mood, asked if I was feeling depressed. Before I could respond and much to my surprise, Drow hit the nail on the head by replying to Prince, "No. It's not that. Peter is like a turtle. He likes to stick his head out and move around a bit. Then he pulls his head back into its shell and enjoys some inwardness. Afterwards he will come out again."

I was very pleased that Drow knew me this well and also that unknowingly he had chosen the very image (a tortoise withdrawing its limbs) which the *Bhagavad Gita* recommends for one aspiring to lead a rich contemplative life. It is not a pattern that is either understood by nor acceptable to most socially-oriented Americans. The most common pattern of life in the United States is moving from desire to willful action, from willful action to either achievement or frustration, and then on to the next desire.

On the platform that evening, waiting for the train that would take Drow to Cochin for a flight out of India and me on to Calicut to rejoin Guru, I told Drow the legend of how Varkala got its name. It seems that one day Indra, the king of the gods, was sitting in his palace in heaven. Suddenly the delicious peace was shattered by the loud bickerings and disputations of some of the lesser gods and goddesses.

In spite of Indra's attempts at mediation, the ruckus went on for days. Finally, fed up with the disturbance, he announced that heaven was not a place for such noisy conflict and therefore he was going to temporarily banish these deities from heaven until they could "get their act together."

He took off his cloak and said, "I will drop my cloak down upon the Earth, and wherever it lands, there I will send all of you. When you have learned to live together peacefully on Earth, you may return to heaven. He dropped his cloak, and Varkala (which is derived from the Sanskrit word for "cloak") is reputed to mark the spot where it landed.

Just as I was finishing this story, our train chugged into

the station. The first class compartment we were assigned was already occupied by a high Catholic bishop and his male and female attendants. All three of them eyed us very warily as we dropped our big backpacks to the floor and shoved them under the seats.

The bishop had a long grey beard and was clad in a floor-length orange robe and a red plaid bill-less cap with tails streaming from it down his back. It was quite a getup for someone who was eyeing our attire up and down disapprovingly. They did not seem consoled that we obviously had two local friends in the form of Prince and Sree Kumar, who were yelping good-byes and best wishes through the bishop's window at us.

At midnight the train pulled into Cochin. Drow and I hugged and bid a hurried, groggy but heartfelt *adieu* to each other, and to an adventure that had been remarkably compressed into four and a half days. I returned to my berth and drifted off to sleep, content in the knowledge that each bump, jostle and lurch was carrying me back to the resumption of my inner and outer work with Guru.

32

Killer Pain
And Pain Killer

The train arrived in Calicut on time at 5:00 AM. From our recent Calicut stay I was familiar enough with the morning ritual at the Narendran home to not want to wake or disturb them so early. So I spread a grass mat on the floor of the station's First Class Waiting Room, and after brushing my teeth and throwing water on my face in the smelly bathroom, I settled down to read a play by Tagore.

At 6:30 I took an auto-rickshaw through the reddening dawn and watched as the green jungle foliage seemed to materialize out of a vaporous void. The day was mainly spent in a delicious solitude which I lapped up like a thirsty beast. I bathed, shaved, washed clothes, ate a delicious breakfast of light airy *idlis* and a creamy coconut sauce, wrote several letters, read, began the journal report of my days with Drow, and had brief individual conversations with each family member.

Guru arrived from Vythiri in the afternoon while I was out shopping. It was great to see him. Not only did he look rested and recharged, but coming into his presence was like entering a cool pool of clear water: The contours of Self which one could make out at the depths, not being obscured by the surface agitations of an ego, turn out to be the common Self pulsating at the heart of all life.

This is the universal attraction of a true guru and what differentiates this phenomena from the ordinary deification of other celebrities. When one glorifies a guru, it is actually one's very own Self that is being acknowledged and celebrated. In fact, the essential function of a guru is to remove the veil of ignorance and the conditioned projections obscuring the realization of one's true Self and its identity with the All. As a consequence of the vision transmitted by the guru, one becomes liberated from all internal and external hindrances to one's unique actualization of the Self.

Guru gave a class and dictated some more for the book he is writing. We had dinner, chatted and joked, totally oblivious to the crisis and pain that lay in waiting just around the corner.

The next morning, as Guru was straightening up from the Indian style (squatting) toilet, he was struck down with the crippling pain of a freak vertebral injury. Only with great effort was he able to drag himself out of the bathroom to call for help. With some difficulty he was put on his bed where he spent the day wriggling in pain. That evening, like a football player who insists upon reentering the fray even after an injury, Guru insisted on honoring his commitment to speak to the philosophy students of the Calicut Arts and Science College.

It is said that "Philosophy doesn't bake any bread," but at least for Guru, philosophy is the best painkiller. During the ninety minutes of his discourse, he himself was lost in the vision he was presenting. He carried his audience with him through several millennia of the high and systematic thinking of India's great philosophers in their attempt to discover and describe the origin, dynamics and meaning of life. He concluded with the present challenge of creating a philosophy that is not a rival to any other philosophy but which is comprehensive enough to embrace the validity of all points of view. He suggested it also serve as a foundation for the reenfranchisement of the many oppressed people in present day global society. Such a philosophy should serve as a guide for spiritual liberation. In this sense, even more so than in the sense of being a distraction from aggravated nerve endings, philosophy has the potential of being the ultimate antidote to pain and suffering.

When Guru finished, I was asked to address the gathering. Knowing that Guru would be needing to lie down soon, I kept my comments very brief. I noted the balance implied in the college name (Arts and Science). I stated my hope that they didn't approach those two fields as bodies of information to be studied from books.

I reiterated the words uttered hundreds of years ago by a Dominican monk, Meister Eckhart, "It is not that the artist is a special kind of person, but rather that each person is a special kind of artist." Each of us is forever writing the script of our own life drama as well as creating worlds for others to see, experience and ponder. A college Art program should help us make such individual creativity more conscious and purposefully suited to our own deepest inner imperatives.

Science means "knowledge." In India, traditionally knowledge is considered to be of two kinds, *vidya* and *avidya*. The latter (*avidya*) refers to all knowledge which presupposes duality and separation between the knower and what is known. This is referred to as nescience or ignorance. *Vidya*, on the other hand, refers to the knowledge which sees the interior essential unity of all within the one selfsame consciousness. What passes for science in the West, with its absolute insistence on "objectivity" is referred to as ignorance in the East, although today most Indian colleges and universities are aping their Western counterparts.

I concluded with the hope that the goal in both science and art be to gain a greater understanding of the seamless reality lived as "self/world."

As Guru was helped into the car waiting to take us back to Narendren's house, I noted flickers of pain beneath the surface of his kindhearted blessings and reassurances to the well-wishers who gathered around to see him off. We rode through the town at a slow steady speed, and yet I could see his body shiver with an uncontrollable wave of pain with each bump or pothole we encountered.

A reminiscence and foreshadowing crossed my mind. Once, after having a private audience with the Pope, Guru was asked, "Is the Pope a kind man?" Guru's reply was,

"How can anyone say if the Pope is a kind man, really? He has every desire fulfilled and is waited on day and night. Let him go out and live among the people and feel the pains of the common man. Only then will we see if the Pope is a kind man."

The next few days would reveal how Guru would respond to his own physical crisis.

33

The Secret Of Devotion

The next day we were to shift camp to the hilltop gurukula in Kanakamala, sixty kilometers north of Calicut. Although our Calicut hosts pleaded with Guru to stay and rest, he followed a strong intuition that he should make it at least to Jyoti's family house in Tellicherry, very near to Kanakamala. Anandan, Jyoti's father, came in a hired car. Eight of us piled in. It would have been more except for some deference to Guru's delicate condition.

I grew up thinking that sitting "Indian Style" meant sitting cross-legged. Now, after a decade and a half of experience in Indian cars, buses and trains, I think of sitting "Indian Style" as an overlapping compression of human bodies seemingly arranged as a challenge to the principle of "the impenetrability of matter." This phenomenon calls to mind the telephone booth stuffing craze my parents' generation invented during their college days. One culture's fleeting craze is another's pragmatic custom.

On the way to Tellicherry, we passed through a town in which Guru had been scheduled to speak but had sent word in the morning of his cancellation. As we were passing the *ashram* where he was to have spoken, we were flagged down by a crowd of people who, knowing Guru was to pass by but not knowing when, had been standing for two hours in an attitude of reverence and expectation. They circled around the car, bowed in salutation and received Guru's blessing.

In a country like America, such behavior could be seen as infantile, servile and demoralizing. Yet I have come to realize that in this context, quite the opposite is true. The true beneficiaries of such intense devotion are the devotees themselves. For Guru such displays of devotion as this and the continual procession of people wishing to touch his feet can be very inconvenient and intrusive. But the inner dynamic at work within the devotee is that in such acts each one is tuning oneself to resonate with and in fact resemble the highest qualities which that devotee is attributing to the divine object of devotion.

It is impossible to show true reverence to Guru, for example, as a representative of the highest wisdom, without acknowledging within oneself the existence, substance and meaning of that wisdom. Wisdom is considered as the common inheritance of all, and divinity as the source and Self of all. Therefore in reverencing wisdom and worshiping divinity, the devotee, even if only subconsciously, is elevating his or her own self and in the process undergoes a subtle transformation of attunement.

It is this dynamic, which operates each of the thousands of times a year someone touches his feet, that leads Guru each time to mutter, "Narayana," the name denoting the indwelling God or Spirit in all, in the toucher as well as the touched. When I asked him about this practice, he said the implied meaning is, "Oh, God, why are you touching me when you are equally there?"

His own guru, Nataraja Guru, used to say, "My role is only that of a postman. The devotee is posting a message at my feet, which I should immediately pass along to God." This he did by also saying, "Narayana."

Recently a reporter asked Guru how it feels to be called "Guru." He replied, "It seems like calling a postman, 'Post Office.' A postman is not the post office. Similarly I, at best, am just a representative of the wisdom of guruhood, which is far more vast than this finite person here."

It's a hazy bright morning during my initial visit to India.

The dust from the parade of school children marching past the gurukula gate has settled. The echoes of their cheerful chatter are yielding to a caressing silence. Carrying empty cloth sacks, Vijayan (a new Indian friend) and I are strolling into town to purchase vegetables for the gurukula kitchen.

In the distance I see a small temple shrine a few feet off the road. Although I have never passed this way before, something is hauntingly familiar about the structure. Usually I am not particularly moved by the symbolic forms of religious sentiment, but I feel drawn to this shrine.

Following my gaze and sensing my interest, Vijayan gently breaks the silence. "That temple has a very special history and significance. Narayana Guru was our teacher's teacher. At the time when he was alive, caste prejudices and restrictions were very strong. A large portion of the population was branded as 'untouchable.' In addition to other indignities, they were barred from entering temples of worship. Although Narayana Guru was not of this downtrodden caste, his sympathy and boundless identity with all life caused him to feel personally the sting of this injustice.

"Rather than expressing his outrage through protest and debate, he elected a more positive approach. Going against the objections of even many of his own followers, he initiated and supervised a campaign to build numerous temples, as well as schools and hospitals, that would be open to all. This very temple we are approaching is the first such temple he erected nearly fifty years ago."

We leave our sandals at the entranceway, cross the swept-sand courtyard, and stand before the two doors leading to the inner shrine. I know from previous visits to Hindu temples that the inner shrine houses an altar dedicated to one or another of the Hindu deities. Hindus claim to have thirty-three million gods, each of which has its own divine attributes. There is a goddess of wisdom, a goddess of prosperity, a god of fertility, a god who presides over the senses, and on and on.

As I pause at the passage to the inner sanctum, I try to imagine what it must have felt like to have been an untouchable standing poised to enter a public temple shrine for the first time. I wonder which deity and which divine qualities will be enshrined herein.

I climb the three stone steps and push open the door. Upon a small granite platform is propped a large ornately bordered mirror. Across the bottom of the mirror are three simple Sanskrit words: *TAT TVAM ASI*. THOU ART THAT. We come in search of God, and upon arriving at our destination we discover our own self, smiling or frowning enigmatically back at us.

At Anandan's house we were welcomed with a joy, thickly muted with the sobriety engendered by Guru's condition. A power-outage and the hour of rapidly fading dusk added to the creation of a dark mood. The family members giving orders to one another in exaggeratedly hushed whispers, almost turned the evening somber. Guru soon pierced the gloom with lighthearted joking (sandwiched between muffled moans).

After touching base and hearts with each family member, Guru shooed us out of his room except for two young gurukula men who would look after him in the night. We all found nooks to spread our mats or mattresses to dream, doze, and await the dawning of yet another new day—which like every day would present itself as a mysterious gift, wrapped in the changing pastel hues of dawn, begging to be opened and enjoyed. This anticipation and appreciation of renewal and abundance is a posture I first developed as transmitted by Guru. Now I found myself wondering if he himself would be able to maintain it in the face of his present excruciating physical pain.

34

From The Excruciating To The Exquisite

The journey must have further aggravated Guru's spine. Throughout the night and the next two days, howls of pain echoed through the house at five to ten minute intervals. In the sixteen years I have known Guru, five of which I lived and traveled with him continuously, I have never known him to complain of his own pains or express any signs of personal suffering. The shadow of suffering one could sometimes see pass across his features was always a reflection of his sympathy for the tribulations and predicaments of others. It must have been this previous absence that lent such a haunting quality to these present outbursts.

When I moan, it is the moan of a single individual. But it was as if in the howling of Guru, one could hear the voice of the suffering of all living beings. Equally remarkable was that the flashes of excruciating pain which intermittently shook his body seemed to leave absolutely no trace in his psyche or mood when they passed, just as lightning leaves not a trace on the midnight sky. He remained serenely cheerful. In the middle of telling a story, a flash of pain would cause a spasm to contract his whole body and elicit an uncontrollable shriek. After a few tense moments, his body would again relax, and he would pick up the thread of his story in mid-sentence.

What is more, in between howls he has continued to dictate verses and commentaries overflowing with joy and wonder. While wriggling in excruciating pain, his inner vision and experience has maintained its quality of exquisite clarity and peace, with a consistent undercurrent of a mystical bliss.

In one particularly inspiring class Guru was highlighting and describing the One and Eternal life-force that ingeniously animates all living beings. He began by taking the example of a person at rest and seemingly motionless:

"Within such a person, arteries are carrying blood from the heart to every tissue, to every cell of every muscle, nerve and bone. From all such parts of the organism, veins gather the soiled and depleted blood and bring it back to the heart. With the help of liver, kidney and lungs, impurities are eliminated, and freshly replenished oxygenated blood is recirculated. The food that has gone into the stomach is ingeniously mixed with various kinds of digestive juices and is broken into its finer elements to be carried along with blood to nourish decaying cells and the generation of new cells.

"At the same time, all nerves are keeping vigil to receive stimuli at their receptor end. Upon receiving the stimulus, a message is immediately conveyed to the brain. The motor system is kept in constant readiness to receive commands and to give appropriate response to stimuli.

"Just as it is one water that assumes different forms with various names such as ocean, cloud, rain, snow, melting ice and river, similarly the life in a tiger, a lion, a butterfly, a mosquito, a tree, and a man or woman is the same. Taking the example of a tree—from underneath the earth the roots gather water mixed with nutrients such as acids and alkalies, salts and minerals which are zealously carried to the very tip of the sprouting new growth at the end of the tree's branches. In return the solar energy absorbed by the leaves is transformed into chlorophyll and deposited in the green banks of the leaves. From this open kitchen of the tree, nourishment is carried to every tissue in the trunk, both bark and pith, and flows to the smallest capillaries of the roots, whereby the tree lives just as we human beings live.

"In the life referred to here, we see the intelligent functioning of our individual programmer. When each life is set to manifest in a certain manner in a certain body, it keeps itself loyal to the physical, chemical, biological and even psycho-sociological laws which are assigned for the proper functioning of that particular organism. In spite of the variegation of the outer mode, the spirit in all is one, and it persists even beyond physical death and destruction. That Being, which is the subtle essence, this whole world has as its self. That is the Real. That is One and Eternal. You are That!" (Howls of pain omitted).

I listened to Guru's words and pondered over them in the context of the immense inner peace he was exhibiting even in the face of nerve-wracking pain. It struck me he was saying, and indeed demonstrating, that spiritual peace is not so much something to be created and developed as it is simply to be discovered and accepted. However one may seek to explain it, the very essence of peace seems to be something that we absorb, something that comes like a gift, a given, in the very depth of our being. There is something abundantly peaceful at the core of existence. This same existence is at the core of human nature as well.

In daily life this "given" is veiled by countless distractions and distorted by innumerable errors. This is why all spiritual disciplines from diverse traditions throughout the world and ages have emphasized a persistent process of self-recollection and a very gentle merging with the depth of one's own being as the pathway to spiritual peace.

Along these lines, which all merge in the peace of the Self, there are countless variations on the theme. Some traditions recommend chanting, others breathing exercises, some "just sitting," some an approach to activity which treats ends and means non-dualistically. Some traditions advocate a rigorous examination of questions such as "Who am I?" Others recommend dancing. Some prescribe devotional exercises where ultimately the boundaries melt between the worshiper and the object of worship.

Whatever the technique or practice, the value implicit is the same: 1) The dissolution of all illusory boundaries between self and other, which give rise to the apparent struggle for existence of seemingly separate beings, and 2) a resolution of all into the peace of the one eternal and infinite Self.

Another of Guru's morning classes made the connections between peace, wonder, gratitude and love very clear to me. Imagine the following coming from one immobilized with crippling pain:

"Why the universe? Even the face of a child epitomizes the cosmic wonder that is never the same for two moments. One moment the child is tearfully crying, and before the teardrop dries, the child is mirthfully laughing. Did God learn changing moods from the child, or is the child mimicking God's sportive drama?

"I could have been a clod of earth, insensitive to my surroundings, but my Lord has given me five senses, and each one is receptive to a thousand shades of perceptual beauty. He (the reference here is to Lord Siva, the King of the Cosmic Dance) has given me this coordinated mind which can weave the empirical illusions and my poetic dreams into a tapestry of the most magical excellence. It is with gratitude that I acknowledge that He sits behind my eyes and sees His cosmic vision, sits behind my ears and listens to the choir of the spheres.

"I don't have the drudgery of religion. He does not expect me to undergo the tedium of reading heavy books nor of listening to the arguments of great pundits. I have only to keep my senses open and my mind attuned to His presentation. I am told the scriptures are revealed books of wisdom. To me this grand world is written in a common language and illustrated with the living figures of the changeful world. This is more than a revealed scripture.

"Life has its thorns and flowers, mornings and evenings, days and nights, sweet dreams and nightmares, jubilation and moments of wretchedness, plenty and poverty. Like a wizard, the Lord changes the scenario from the brightest to the darkest and back again to the brightest.

Unlike a scientist, who is always pestering his or her little brain with questions such as, 'What causes which and what for,' I do not torture my logic-generating mind. Thus the Lord is ever-pleased to fill my mind instead with the never-ceasing narration of His drama, the painting of His pictures and the projection of His fairy tales.

He is the most central figure merrily dancing all the time as a joyous elf. I am lucky that he has chosen my loveful heart as the stage for his mirthful dance. Thus I am assured of the sweet blessedness which is always with me. When He dances, the world also dances. Then my heart too dances in love and gratitude."

Listening to these and similar poetic effusions was having a profound effect upon me. My own physical pains began to seem secondary and more like goads toward greater wakefulness than the stings of a punishing God or evidences of a faulty body. My emotional fixations took on the appearance of bubbles rising in a well. Life was more grand than a single mind could begin to encompass. My mind's preoccupation with my own melodrama loosened, letting in a flood of impressions of the people around me.

One Indian Family

We have been staying at Jyoti's house for two weeks. To some extent we have been able to erase the burdensome distinction between host and guest and have been living as one family. The nuclear family consists of Sarojini and Anandan (mother and father), Jyoti, Sandhya, Shanti, and Baby (four daughters aged 21-30), Song (five year old granddaughter), and Tittoo (two year old grandson).

Each family member has an easily distinguishable role. Anandan, a lawyer, is breadwinner and alleged patriarch. The fact that the women do *all* the work around the house gives them the *defacto* say-so over what to do, when to do it and how to go about it. Furthermore, I can sense the five females constitute a formidable power block over any issue about which they agree. As a result balance has been established. All the family members respect, serve and truly love Anandan. In return he sees that his directives, for the most part, correspond with the pre-configured wishes and tendencies of the others.

I am reminded of the self-proclaimed "King of the Universe" encountered by the Little Prince in the book of the same title. When asked by the Little Prince how he could possibly rule over the entire universe, the king said something to the effect of, "It's easy. I simply make sure that my commands correspond perfectly with the nature of my subjects. For example, in the morning I command the sun to rise, and in the evening I command it to set. In this manner

I find I receive 100% obedience from every being in the universe."

Sarojini is the bright-eyed, hard working, actual head of the household. I once asked Guru how such a flagrantly male chauvinist society as India could be considered a matriarchal society. He explained with the following illustrative scenario:

You arrive at a family home and are welcomed by the man of the house, who invites you to take a seat in the parlor. He sits down and joins you. His wife humbly pokes her head into the room and greets you. The man asks her to prepare you both some tea, and she retreats back to the kitchen. The two of you go on talking. The conversation comes to a critical juncture where you are agreeing to embark on some business venture together. Just then from the kitchen comes the sound of a ladle dropping to the floor. Your host clears his throat, excuses himself and leaves the room. Three minutes later he returns, resumes his seat, and again clearing his throat begins, "Uh, well, about that deal we were discussing, I've decided to reconsider. . ."

Sarojini clearly exudes that kind of power, emanating from an inner authority that is first and foremost informed by love. The challenge for a mother with such abundance of love and strength is to avoid crossing the fine line between being supportive and being over-bearing. What begins as the good intention of wanting only what is best for those in one's care can easily transgress into a domineering posture. This danger exists due to the fact that ultimately no one (not even a mother) can decide what is best for another person. Each person is unique in ways which, in the final analysis, only that person can discover for himself or herself.

In general, respect for individual uniqueness is not Indian society's strong suit. There is very little opportunity for a young Indian man or woman to break new ground or explore alternative paths or life styles. Not only are life styles, career paths, caste prejudices, and gender stereotypes watertight, but even the placement within the family, such as eldest son or youngest daughter, can dictate a life of obligation and frustration. An eldest son may be expected to pay for the dowries of all sisters and the education of all younger brothers. The youngest daughter will be expected to postpone marriage until all elder sisters have been "married off," as it is called.

In the West, young boys and girls have recently won wide acceptance for premarital sexual intercourse. In India, even premarital *social* intercourse is taboo. An innocent conversation with a boy could ruin a teenage girl's reputation and prospects for marriage. Almost all marriages are still arranged by the parents, and those marrying by mutual choice, in what are called (perish the thought), "love marriages," are ostracized as black sheep. Immediately after completing one's studies, a girl should get a job and support the family or else get married. A man should do both. Immediately after marriage a bride is usually put in the house and under the dominance of the mother-in-law.

For the most part, caste heritage determines the type of work one will be considered fit for. Prejudicial stereotypes are so pervasive that even if the highest wisdom of spiritual insight is spoken by a mason, carpenter, or plumber, it will be dismissed as of no value; whereas if an engineer or doctor speaks utter nonsense, it will be accepted as gospel.

To some extent this particular family has shown itself capable of breaking with tradition by the fact that Jyoti, the eldest daughter, is permitted to leave home, forsaking both job and marriage, to live, travel, study with and attend upon Guru. Jyoti is a very bold soul whose courage is in ironic contrast to her petite body. She has a very high voice, and her speech is constantly punctuated with laughter. Almost anything can become a joke for her. No one can take themselves or the situation too seriously around her. She has a special intuitive knack with Guru and seems able to anticipate his needs often before he himself has registered them.

Many friends, and family members too, have warned Jyoti that her extreme emotional attachment to Guru may cause her a problem *vis a vis* living a life of her own further down the line. But through her own nonconformity and creativity in relations with others, she is forging an independence that should serve her well. Since she is studying Guru's teaching, there is the hope that she may integrate the elements of nonattachment implied in the discipline before her attachment is seriously threatened.

Sandhya is the next eldest and the first married. I attended her wedding six years ago. Guru was conducting the ceremony, and I will never forget his unlikely opening statement to all who had gathered, "As a rule, I advise all friends who come to me for advice and teaching that they avoid marriage if it is at all possible." That is certainly not the kind of benediction one expects at a wedding, and I always have wondered how Sandhya and Sashi, her bridegroom, felt about it.

Sandhya is presently eight months pregnant with her second child. She seems to be gently coaxing it into shape with her meditation. Much of the day she sits rapt in contemplation, seemingly in communion with both her offspring-to-be and their common Maker. For the most part, the others refuse her attempts to join in the considerable housework, allowing her just enough participation to feel she remains a contributing presence. In fact, her mere "brooding" presence is contribution enough.

Song, her five year old daughter, is an impish precocious girl. She delights in delivering long-winded Malayalam orations to each and all of the four Americans here. She is unwilling to believe we could be so unintelligent as to not understand her. In fact, we each feel compelled to nod in complete agreement with whatever she says. In return Ramana, Penelope's fifteen year old American son, has discovered Song is also amenable to and proficient at mimicking entire English sentences with total conviction, though she knows the meaning of only a handful of English words.

Shanti, the third daughter, is very sincere and somewhat shy. I think her serious manner may stem in part from a couple of mobility and sight threatening diseases she struggled with and triumphed over in her early years. Another source of weight upon her psyche is that the bulk of the housework falls on Shanti's strong shoulders, with Jyoti off with Guru, Sandhya married and now pregnant again, and Baby studying full time. Water is to be drawn from the well for kitchen, toilet and cleaning needs; clothes and bedding are to be washed, rinsed, hung up to dry, and folded, all by hand; three elaborate meals a day are to be prepared over gathered dried palm frond, wood and coconut husk fires; floors are to be swept and scrubbed; and so on.

It breaks my heart to see the horizon of a young woman in her twenties narrowed to this extent. In the two weeks we have been here I have only seen her leave the house twice, once to go to a movie and once to go to typing class. Both times she was dressed up beautifully, like Cinderella on her way to the ball.

From all this, it should not be imagined Shanti goes around glum or grumpy. She is always ready with a genuine smile. Cheerful resignation is a national character trait of India, just as its opposite, assertive individualism, is a national character trait in America.

Baby, as her nickname implies, is the youngest. She is twenty-one and presently studying for a Master's Degree in English Literature. Perhaps that explains why, of the four daughters, she seems the most westernized in temperament, taste and sensibility. She is affectionate, playful, poetic and somewhat dreamy. Her burden (I hope to discover whether she experiences it as such) is that circumstances and her own decision to pursue higher studies make her heir-apparent to assume financial responsibility for the family, after her father's impending retirement. This is confounded by the facts that in India teaching positions are hard to come by, low paying, and unbelievably require a buy-in bribe fee the equivalent of over two year's salary. Although the future is casting a shadow, I think Baby is pretty good about living in the present and enjoys the intellectual stimulation and social interchange which her college program offers.

I asked each daughter the following question: "If you had one wish *for yourself* regarding your future, what would it be?" Their answers were as follows:

JYOTI: I never think of the future. But if I have to think like that, then let Guru live a long life, free from suffering, and let me always be with him.

SANDHYA: I want good health. I am too often sick.

SHANTI: Let everything I do bring happiness to those around me, and may no other suffer because of me.

BABY: Whatever comes may come. I don't have any such wish as you suggest. [Then when pressed:] The one thing I do care about is that I should get a job teaching in a college. If I get a job, then I know everything else will be alright.

36

Yoga
As Consolation Prize

The Anandan family has not only opened its home and heart to Guru for the period of his treatment and recovery. His present contingent, consisting of a half dozen young men, Penelope and her children (Ramana and Aruna), and myself have also been welcomed. The first two or three days we were treated like guests—brought tea, called for meals and even sometimes having well-water drawn for baths. In situations like this I am always guided by the perceptive Japanese proverb, "Fish and guests both begin to stink after three days."

Accordingly after breakfast on the third morning, I washed my own and a few extra dishes, an act which would have been vigorously denied a "guest." In this case there was only genuine surprise and token protest, made mainly to give me an out if I was not sincere. Then before leaving the kitchen, I requested a knife, cutting board, vegetables and instructions. Thus my status officially changed from guest to extended family member.

In the evening Guru called the whole family into his room and announced that in spite of spending three days in their house, he had rarely seen any of them because of their work in the kitchen, etc. Therefore he was proclaiming the next day a holiday for them, during which the kitchen would be off-limits. The Indian visitors volunteered to prepare breakfast and lunch, and the four Americans offered to fix dinner.

The next morning I went into town to buy butter, noodles,

peanuts, yogurt and vegetables at the market. That evening it somehow took the four of us nearly three hours, but we managed to put together an "exotic" meal of vegetables sauteed in butter, mixed with an Indonesian-type peanut sauce, over noodles, with a mint-cucumber-yogurt salad on the side. It was relished by all except for one Malayalee man who would not touch it.

From that day onward, the visitors (particularly the Indians) have assumed a much more active role in the kitchen. Penelope regularly washes large loads of dishes, pots, pans, cups and glasses, etc. And I try to make a routine of helping chop vegies for the midday meal.

Each morning an Ayurvedic physician comes to treat both Guru and myself. He is an elderly man with strong oversized hands. The main treatment consists of massages with hot-packs dipped in boiling herbally medicated oil. According to Guru, Ayurveda massage is mainly intended for the application of the oils in such a way so as to stimulate the growth of new tissue. The tissue thus stimulated may take up to three months to grow to the extent that the positive impact and recovery is experienced. It's a far cry from the quick-fix of surgery, but I've been suffering for nine months with this pain, and I'm willing to give this a try.

Guru has been improving slowly but steadily. He still needs help getting up and down in bed and has to be supported to get to the bathroom, but now he can sit up in a chair for up to about forty-five minutes.

A different Ayurvedic doctor who examined me three weeks ago in Parur recommended I sleep only flat on my back and not at all on my sides. A medical doctor here told me I should sleep only on my side and not at all flat on my back. At first this contradiction confounded and disturbed me, until I hit upon a very agreeable solution. When I feel like lying on my back, I think of the Ayurvedic doctor and her advice, and when I feel the need to shift over to one or another side, I think of the medical doctor and his advice. Thus I rest easy, always having the feeling of following a doctor's orders.

Given the possibility of viewing my positions as deviations rather than fulfillments, I am also forced to recognize this as another case of seeing a glass as "half full" as opposed to seeing the same as "half empty." I am beginning to think that we are presented that choice (half full vs. half empty) moment after moment, and the choice is as significant as that implied in Hamlet's "To be or not to be."

One afternoon when several of us were sitting around in Guru's room fretting over his condition, he aroused us out of our listlessness with the provocative question, "What is yoga?" I responded that yoga means "union," to which he replied, "That's right but union of what with what?"

We went around the room and each of us suggested what we thought was united through yoga. Some of our answers were:

1) ends and means (In this sense yogic action would be action performed for its own sake and not for any future reward.)

2) the mind and the Self (Another way of putting this would be the union of the surface modifications of the mind with the mind's undisturbed depths)

3) the personal individuated self with the Universal Self (Here the individual self is relative, that is it relates to that which is other than or outside itself; whereas the Universal Self is absolute in that it is all-encompassing, and hence there is nothing "other" to which it can relate.)

4) the seer and the seen (This implies that even when one supposes one is relating to something external, one's immediate experience is always of modifications of one's own consciousness, one's own self.)

Guru listened intently and approved of each suggestion. After everyone had their turn he offered the following summation:

"The eternally present substratum of the self, which persists through all modulations is Existence, Awareness, and Affectivity. When the self is experienced as relative and confined within a body, the affectivity can range from agonizing pain to orgasmic pleasure and all shades in between. But when the self is known in its ever-abiding foundational aspect, there is a persistent awareness of imperturbable existence which is in itself unalterably blissful.

"Yoga, however it be approached, is finally this immortal existential awareness of self-founded bliss. In fact, it is glimpses of this same bliss at the heart of the Self which all of us have experienced in moments of peace and contentment (being at one with oneself) and ecstasy and wonder (being at one with others, one's world, and the Great Mystery).

"Both desire and fear imply a sense of deficiency and insecurity on the one hand, and a projected 'otherness' on the other hand. Knowing the identity between one's self and the Absolute, spells fearlessness and desirelessness.

"Wholeness is not something yet to be achieved through satisfying desire after desire. Rather it is to be realized in the depth of one's soul as the basic reality of one's own self. That self is the connecting link with 'others,' the thread running through and uniting the many into one. That is the union referred to as yoga."

Speaking those words, he closed his eyes with the hint of a beatific smile on his face. He asked to be helped to roll over onto his other side from where he slipped into a peaceful sleep. We looked at each other, wondering what had just happened. Here, we had come into this man's sickroom feeling sorry for him and intending to console him in some manner. Instead he had taken pity on our sagging spirits and, while involving us in the process, managed to lift those spirits to pleasantly soaring heights. We virtually floated out of the room, only seeming to go our separate ways.

37

Fluctuations Of Joy

My taurine nesting instinct has manifested here as a comfortable nook at the far end of the long veranda spanning the outside of the second story of this brick and teakwood house. The veranda is covered by a sloping tile roof and is enclosed on three sides. The front, facing the road, is completely open from floor to roof, except for three Romanesque columns. The varied jungle foliage grows within feet of the veranda-long opening. Creeping vines have even wrapped themselves around the columns. It is the best marriage of indoors/outdoors I have ever experienced.

Propped up in my bed, I get a 3-D cinerama view of the subtly changing hues and moods of the greenery. Lying on my stomach with my head at the foot of the bed, I can watch the procession of passersby on the narrow dirt road in front of the house. They, in turn, never fail to steal a glance upward to see what I or the other foreigners are up to.

The sounds are diverse, ranging from cricket choirs and warbling bird symphonies to howling dogs and drunkards stumbling home. But by far the most persistent element of this soundtrack has been the arguments, playful shoutings and laughter of children playing cricket from morning to dusk in the small clearing just a dozen coconut palms past the road.

After the first day or two the novelty wore off, and I began to find the constant racket (of children screaming) annoying. But on the fifth morning, in the faint light before dawn, that annoyance was transformed. I was gazing out across the road at the unusually empty and quiet little clearing. I had the distinct feeling the ground or very earth of the clearing was also waking up from nighttime's slumber. There was an almost palpable sense of eager anticipation, of the ground awaiting the arrival of the children, as if it found the pounding of their feet as pleasing as a massage or the tickling fingers of a loved one.

Of course, these sensations may have been originating within myself, but if so were emanating from a part of myself which in my annoyance had remained hidden. I feel something in me was identifying with the organic and sentient nature of this earth, which we mistakenly conceive as being inert in spite of all the signs of life it projects and supports.

After that, I observed the children with a new sense of acceptance. They were no longer "those boys" in "that clearing," but in a strange way they felt like "my boys," and they were in a sense playing "in me." Now every day I'm learning a little more about each of their personalities, as well as the rules and strategy of the game of cricket.

There is a Japanese haiku which simply and poignantly describes this phenomenon:

> When I think of it
> As my snow, how light it feels
> On my bamboo hat.

Yesterday morning in class, after having been told how much we had appreciated our discussion about yoga, Guru gave us a homework assignment. He suggested that throughout the next twenty-four hours, we each observe the fluctuations in our experience of happiness or the lack thereof and reflect upon the nature of happiness and its determining factors. The following is what I noted:

I. DURING CLASS—peace, contentment, a sense of everything (including myself) being in its place. I felt a certitude that both the source and validity of this feeling would remain even in times of its being veiled, ignored or forgotten. I felt a renewed dedication to make my life's goal the establishment of my self in this poised center and to aid others in doing the same.

II. AT LUNCH – I felt rushed, as if I needed to eat fast in order to get my share of the delicious vegetable dishes which had been prepared. I enjoyed the food (and indeed had plenty), but felt that my focus had definitely shifted away from the blissful center experienced during class.

III. SITTING IN SHADE WITH BOOK – I settled down; contentment returned. I wondered why I ever leave this inner center. What disturbance, what erroneous pain-pleasure conditioning can make me get up off my inner throne and chase after phantoms? Of course, there are necessities such as hunger, thirst, toilet, cold, sleep, etc. What about all the rest of the time? And can't all of it, including the necessities, be attended to without losing touch with one's ever-contented imperturbable center?

Aha! That must be how *tyaga* works. Tyaga is the yogic discipline of performing action without attachment to the benefit or fruit of action. Tyaga is said to lead to the maintenance of inner peace. Conversely, *atyagraha* is action prompted by benefit-motive and is said to be the destroyer of our peace. As soon as one is seeking some reward, recognition or other benefit from an action, one has relinquished one's hold on the self-founded peace of one's own soul. Conversely, any action can be performed with a sense of joy if one has not renounced one's eternal self-sufficiency to go like a beggar looking for something else.

IV. SWEEPING THE FLOORS – I was still feeling absorbed in the peace of my Self, until my back started aching. The brooms here consist of a bundle of twigs about three feet long tightly bound at the upper end. Hence one must bend over while sweeping. I tried to remind myself that what affects this body need not touch my inner self-feeling, but I couldn't really extricate my mind from returning again and again to the physical complaint. I sure would love to learn how to detach from physical pain and discomfort.

V. WRITING IN THE EARLY MORNING SUN—Writing about peace, peace returned. Then Aruna walked by telling somebody that she, Ramana, and Penelope were having some tender coconut juice in their room. My immediate reaction was to drop everything and go after some. Then I realized that this was a perfect example of compulsive chasing around after things when otherwise I am fine and communing with my own depth (which melts into a universal depth). I restrained myself and soon forgot all about it, returning to my inner dialogue.

A while later, Aruna appeared before me like an angel, offering me a glass of juice. The heavens rolled open. I would never have enjoyed the drink one tenth as much if I had gone after it. This strikes me as another "law of our inner nature." When things fall to us unsought, they have more value somehow and a more profound impact of wonder and gratitude than when we manipulate things and people to get what we want. Maybe this is because the former come to us with the stamp of Benevolent Grace, which is itself the Gift surpassing all gifts. Such unsought pleasures have the fingerprints, as it were, of that same mysterious Unseen Hand. From the instant a sperm coupled with an egg, this Unseen Hand has been guiding our physiological, biological, and equally well our social, psychological and spiritual development. This line of thinking runs contrary to the conventional "wisdom" in the West that fruits are sweeter when struggled for. Of course when, as in the West, the separate individual ego is seen as the ultimate, then competition and struggle become high values.

Finally Ramana walked by and asked rhetorically, "Isn't it a beautiful morning?" I agreed and mused that at this moment beauty is the inner quality of my experience, and whatever I turn my attention to, be it Ramana himself, the weather, the lush green grass, the sound of children, the ochre colored robes on the line, the smell of the kitchen fires, myself, etc. are all drenched in that beauty.

That beauty, though reflected outside, has an inner source. It is significant that the Hebrew word from which we derive the English "eye" is *ayin*, which literally means "fountain." May we each discover that fountain source within us and bathe the very next person we see, in its beauty.

38

Waning With The Moon

About midway through our two week stay here at Jyoti's house, I undertook my monthly fast which has become something of a ritual for me during the past fifteen years. During my first visit to India (1971), I celebrated Mahatma Gandhi's birthday by going to a local library and reading some of his writings. In one book I read he was writing how everything in nature waxes and wanes, rises and falls, fills and empties, alternately. He suggested that one way to tune oneself to these cyclic rhythms is to observe a fast with each new moon, a symbolic emptying of oneself in solidarity with the "empty moon," after which presumably one would then wax along with the moon.

This idea appealed to me, especially since I had gained a deep appreciation for the phases of the moon during my recent stays in the caves of Crete and on the beach in Goa. Further, I liked the health implications of a periodic day of giving the digestive system a cleansing rest and the emotional-spiritual implications of allowing oneself to sustain the feeling of hunger periodically to gain a more conscious understanding of the miracle of nourishment—the energy it gives us and the anguish from which it saves us.

When asked about fasting, Narayana Guru came up with the great line, "It is better to eat and think about God, than to fast and think about food." How true! I find the one day a month I fast (and inevitably think about food) really helps me to appreciate God (or Nature or Chance) during the other twenty-seven days of the lunar month while eating food. Also each month I renew my appreciation for the sage quote of my friend, Johnny Stallings, "Why do they call it a 'fast' when it goes so 'slow'? "

The same day while fasting, I received a letter from Carolyn. Although I had thought myself beyond grieving, I began to cry. She wrote of her continued love for me, suggesting nothing had changed other than the physical distance between us.

I tried unsuccessfully to figure out just what my tears meant. Maybe I didn't believe her. Maybe I believed her, and it sounded so trivialized. Maybe it reminded me of the tragi-comic lyrics, "How can I miss you when you won't go away." Or maybe I even believed her and was moved to tears by her sincerity. Four very different interpretations of my tears, and yet which one was correct didn't seem to matter.

Guru once suggested, "It's not that we cry because we're sad, but rather that we're sad because we cry." The implication of this contention is that crying can be seen simply as a conditioned psychosomatic response and, as such, need not disturb the thread of our inner well-being. I am realizing emotional independence does not imply achieving a state of constant pleasure. Rather emotional independence implies a deeper sense of self-identity which remains unaffected by the inevitable ebbs, flows and whirlpools of our emotional nature.

Instead of saying, "I am happy" or "I am sad," the Malayalees say, "*Sukham unda* (Happiness is there)" or "*Dukham unda* (Suffering is there)." The difference is subtle yet profound. The Western approach implies some substantial transformation of the self, whereas the Indian perspective implies a deep unmoved substratum of self which simply acknowledges the alternating presence of shifting emotional tones. With a still-fragile sense of detachment, I acknowledged the presence of sadness as I set the letter aside.

Usually during a fast I will consult the *I Ching*. Through a process of tossing three coins six times, a reading is received which is supposed to be specifically relevant to the moment of consultation. Once again I found the relevance to be striking in light of the focus of Guru's recent classes and assignments, as well as my confusion regarding Carolyn's letter. The passage that came up for me was entitled "Return." An excerpt will suffice to give a flavor of what it presented:

> Return, applied to character formation, contains various suggestions. The light principle returns. The counsel is to turn away from the confusion of external things, turning back to one's inner light. There in the depths of the soul, one sees the Divine, the One. It is indeed only germinal, no more than a beginning, a potentiality, but as such clearly to be distinguished from all objects. To know this One means to know oneself in relation to the cosmic forces. For this One is the ascending force of life in nature and in man.

39

Life And Death Valley

My cassette tape player has become very popular here, lending me a faint reflected glory by association. Each evening after Prayer (meditation, chanting and the reading out of Guru's dictation from that day), there is a minor rush to my corner to see who will get first crack at the stereo headphones.

Of the few tapes that I brought, I have discovered the right one for each person's taste. Baby has become a big fan of Paul Simon. Kasmin's taste runs more to the peaceful side, so I play Mark Knopfler's instrumental soundtracks for him. Under my coaching, teenage Ramana has blossomed into a full-fledged Dead Head (fan of the Grateful Dead). And Shanti practically swoons just thinking of her nightly dose of Dire Straits, which seems to take her far away to a world where kitchens and washbasins are unknown.

For most of the Indians this is the first experience of stereo headphones. They are obviously entranced by the effect of being both surrounded by and filled with the music. In the mornings I've been unplugging the headphones, attaching the small auxiliary speaker and serenading all with "Satori," the meditative Japanese bamboo flute music of Riley Lee, and the "New Age" piano composition called "The Miracle of the Dolphins" by Paul Lloyd-Warner.

In a loosely related note, the other morning Giridharan, one of Guru's Malayalee students and a dear friend, approached me and began deciphering the lettering, "Grateful

Dead" on my T-shirt. He at first looked puzzled. He was familiar with both words but was having difficulty putting them together. Suddenly his face lit up with understanding, and he exclaimed, "Ah yes. If it is to be the good finishing, it must be only like that." And he danced away as if he had just learned a great lesson. India has its *Upanishads* and *Yoga Sastras*; America has its *T-shirts* and *Bumper Stickers*.

Yesterday I received a letter which reminded me that T-shirts and bumper stickers are not the only source of wisdom in America. It was from my sixteen year old stepdaughter, Rachel, in California. Along with the letter, she enclosed a copy of her journal, written for her high school English class about a three day outing the entire class took. For a class project, they went into the California desert of Death Valley. Each student spent two of those days and nights completely off on their own in the desert's immense solitude. Their main assignment was simply to observe themselves and their surroundings, and as a secondary assignment, they were given the question to ponder, "Is anybody out there?"

Rachel's journal was moving and beautiful. In it she spoke of dealing with and overcoming various fears, of the sweet fruits of time alone, of the "mystery and magic" of the desert, of the positive quality of its silence, of the enlivening affect of the awareness of one's own inevitable death, and of her sleepless final night disturbed by critters and an eerie wind.

What an experience for a teenager to undergo! I feel compelled to include here a couple of brief passages from her journal. She is describing her first night alone, during which she slept fitfully and awoke often:

> ". . . I just told myself that there was nothing I could do about it if something were going to happen to me, and I might as well try to sleep rather than stay up worrying about it. That helped. I just put myself in the hands of whatever is out there and trusted that I would be okay, and I am."

And later:

> "I don't really know if I can honestly say, if anybody's out there? I believe that there is some higher spirit that watches over us and is out there somewhere, but that is just my belief. I guess more than anything, I will come out of this with more questions. I don't know that anybody can answer that question, 'Is anybody out there?' except for themselves. Each person has their own beliefs about it, and a part of what is out there is a part of each one of us. It is a hard question, and who knows if it can even be answered."

My letter of response to Rachel is reproduced here:

> Very Dear Rachel,
> Your journal was exquisite, filled with many of the qualities I have come to admire and love in you—modesty, sense of wonder, honesty, thoughtfulness, sensitivity, courage, intelligence, openness and unassuming spirituality.
>
> There is only one possible "correction," or rather amendment, I would like to suggest. You referred to your return to the pressures of school and the demands of work as getting back to "reality." Just because we spend more time involved in and thinking about school, work, social-life, etc., than we do with the vastness, solitude and peace of the desert, doesn't make the former "real" and the latter "unreal."
>
> The very nature of most of our worldly concerns is that they are always changing—here today and gone tomorrow—and no sooner do we think we have gotten hold of something, than it slips away and is replaced by another short-lived concern. This total unreliability is the very definition of the *unreal*.
>
> The beneficent and healing silence, on the other hand, is an eternal factor. Though the colors and patterns of the landscape are forever subtly changing, the

awe-inspiring beauty that you discovered within you as mirrored in the desert is also constant. Even when you forget or ignore it in the hubbub of your other interests, it remains reliably there, always awaiting the return of your conscious appreciation. That wondrous vast Beingness you communed with and reflected upon in the desert is Reality. That is the hidden inmost self of all—infinite and eternal. Rachel, you are That.

The fun is that this need not reduce your appreciation of your social life, but rather your vision of the underlying reality means you don't have to take your own melodrama too seriously and can enjoy it for what it is—a passing show, like the sunsets or floating clouds of the desert.

With You In Love
& In Love With You,
Peter

40

The Benevolent Dictator

The past seven days all roles and experiences have become secondary to my role as stenographer. Guru, upon realizing that I would be leaving India shortly, resolved that before my departure he would complete the book he has been dictating to me. The book will consist of his translations and commentaries on 100 verses composed by his teacher's teacher (who is thereby my "great grand-guru").

Working on the book almost daily for these previous sixty days that I have been with him, we have completed approximately half the verses. That leaves an equal number to be accomplished in ten days. Accordingly, we set the goal of five verses a day. That's five separate dictation sessions per day, each one lasting for an hour or more. It is fortunate that the Ayurvedic herbal medicine the physician has me taking for my sciatica is also indicated for, among other ailments, "writer's cramp."

Much of the time Guru very graciously speaks slowly, allowing me time not only to get the words on paper but to do some preliminary editing for syntax and grammar. But often as he goes deep into himself to divine certain profundities and commune with his Muse, he becomes lost to the outer world and speaks rapidly, as if to capture each image before it flees and gives way to the next.

At such times I feel like a verbal pack-mule, straining to keep up. Aside from the pain in my wrists and fingers and the frustration with my clumsy pace, I have almost no understanding, much less appreciation, for what is being written. Sometimes in a flash I even attribute this to the dictation rather than to the dictatee, as in "Hey, this isn't making any sense at all." Invariably when the race is over and I read the dictation back to Guru, I am surprised to discover its rich value and illuminating meaning.

I have come to understand this phenomenon in terms of the current theories on the two hemispheres of the brain. The recognition and written reproduction of sounds is purely a left-brain function, linear and mechanical. The intuitive appreciation of beauty and meaning and the experience of mystical insight and union are functions of the right hemisphere. During the strain and demands of keeping up with what is being dictated, the left-brain is overwhelmingly active, leaving no time or energy for any right-brain pleasantries. Only when the mechanical function is over and I can sit back with a sense of leisure, does the right-brain kick in with both its aesthetic and transcendent capabilities.

Modern neurological research suggests this theory is correct. Hence a very strong case can be made for the introduction of curricula catering to and cultivating the powers of the right hemispheres of the brains of school children. Currently there exists a dramatically disproportionate emphasis on the training and exercise of the left hemisphere.

The day's first dictation begins between 5:00 and 5:30 in the morning, and the final one may be at 10:00 or 11:00 at night. In between I'm on-call. The very sight of me, even if only as a shadow passing outside the doorway, reminds Guru that he'd better get on with the next verse. Even the universal and compulsory afternoon siesta has become vulnerable to this lofty obsession.

A beneficial side-effect of this role is that it grates on, and thereby softens, my ego. Sometimes I feel like the first generation of the developing technology of voice-activated typewriters. The *I Ching* has shed light on this present state of affairs with a ringing aptness:

Your individuality at this time is totally eclipsed by social considerations. In your personal relationships you are thought of in terms of your role and how you manage to fulfill it. Your subordination to this role is an unrewarding moment in your emotional life, but it will pass. Don't force the issue...Remain passive for now and hold to the enduring aspects of the relationship to see you through.

From the hexagram
"Subordinate," R.L. Wing
translation

In fact, Guru is not forcing me to do anything. That issue was settled between us long ago while we were living together in Portland during the first year of our association. Three days a week Guru was teaching a class on *The Bhagavad Gita* at Portland State University. Every evening he was giving talks on "The Psychology of Yoga" at the house where thirteen of us were living with him. One evening after class, he assigned me a project that had to do with creating a map of the world showing the birthplace of various significant philosophical ideas throughout history. For whatever reason, the idea did not appeal to me at all. Throughout that night I wrestled with the problem of whether or not I should undertake the project in spite of my total lack of intrinsic motivation to do so.

The next morning I decided to approach Guru directly with my dilemma. I asked him, "If I am to be your 'disciple,' does that mean that I should do whatever you suggest?"

By way of response he offered an interesting analogy. He said, "A guru is like an optometrist. When you go to an optometrist and tell him or her that you want to improve your vision, the optometrist does not say to you, 'Wonderful. I had the same problem, and I found the perfect corrective lenses. Here you take these same lenses.' No, what the optometrist does is to hold lens after lens in front of your eyes, and you determine which ones work for you. Like that, a guru may suggest possibilities after possibilities to you. Only you can decide in the light of which possibilities things take on a clarity and significance for you."

That one encounter has forever freed me from adopting the role of serf and has saved him from being cast by me in the role of despot.

A few days later, Guru picked up the thread again. He said that *all* secondary motivations should be discarded and not just those emanating from external compulsion. A common example of a secondary motivation prompting an action is the desire for recognition and appreciation from others. Guru stated that we should do something well for the joy of doing it well. If others see our good act and appreciate it, that is to their benefit. If others let our kind act go unnoticed, it is their loss. Spiritual well-being begins to grow when we drop the desire for the enjoyment of any fruits of our actions. "Thus long term calculations must give way to values which can be expressed in the present."

Along these same lines there is a verse in the *Bhagavad Gita* which describes the ultimate attainment of yoga as:

> That state where the relational mind attains tranquility
> ...and where also the Self by the Self in the Self enjoys happiness.
>
> (VI. 20)

Commenting on this verse, Nataraja Guru points out that to attain such a state one need not add anything to his or her knowledge or behavior but rather need only remove whatever is extraneous in any situation. All that matters, according to this practice, is one's moment to moment self-identification with whatever one visualizes as the highest value in one's life. This may be conceived as God, the Absolute, Love, Peace, Beauty or whatever. This requires a vigilant contemplative attitude and a willingness to forego the extraneous.

There are other little moments penetrating the bubble of ego and reminding me I am right where I want to be and doing exactly what I need to be doing, in spite of (or maybe because of) the resistance I put up. One such instance occurred during this morning's second dictation. Guru was pausing to gather his thoughts, and mine began to wander.

I thought when the dictation was over, I would walk the kilometer to the nearest junction and buy some bananas, some nut mixture, maybe some bread and butter, and possibly even a pastry. My reverie was interrupted by Guru's next sentence which remarked, "When the palate begins to dictate its terms, man degenerates into an errand boy, forever running around only to please his palate."

Amazed and amused by this striking example of synchronicity or Coincidence, which with a capital "C" is a good enough modern synonym for the Absolute, I decided to forsake the fancied errand and instead remained at the house to write this journal entry.

One morning our book dictation routine was interrupted by the dictation (what else?) of a letter. But that letter, and one written the next morning, so well encapsulate what Guru has lived, learned, taught and modeled during the three weeks of his disability, I have reproduced the essence here.

Our morning dictation was interrupted by the special delivery of a letter from a woman in Singapore reporting that her husband had just had a heart attack and was in serious condition in the hospital. Guru set aside what he was working on and dictated a heartfelt reply:

"Nothing is more natural to a man than allowing his final breath to escape into the open and reverberate with the stratosphere and beyond. But we are so conditioned with the fear of change. Please ask P. to rest his mind in the silence of the Immaculate Light. He and all of us are part and parcel of this One, which never diminishes nor increases. This light is an eye that is never agitated by what it sees. It is described in the *Upanishads* as a bird that sits with another bird of the same plumage on the same tree but which is not tasting of the tree's sweet or bitter fruits.

"I was given a chance these days to look into the wretchedness of the body when it cannot function and to look into the intense pain *prana* can bring to the very matrix of my nervous system which all through my life was giving me so many pleasures of perceptions and imaginations. To stand apart from that marketplace and witness a higher consciousness, not dominated by pain or pleasure, has been a great blessedness."

And then this from a letter dictated the next morning to be sent directly to the ailing man himself:

"I pray that you experience the best an aspirant can upon entering higher consciousness. The lower mind, hitched on to people, objects and events on the phenomenal side, should be unplugged to rise into higher consciousness.

"My attitude toward life and death is probably not the same as many. First of all, I do not feel commissioned to do anything for anyone. The sun shines and the river flows because of their intrinsic nature. Similarly I function according to my nature. It can stop any time. So I do not have to take any extra care to prolong my life. To be in the body was very good. Cessation of that can be even better. My attitude towards a death-bringing disease is one of love and acceptance rather than of horror. So I will not fight a disease. However, I may accept measures that may relieve me of unnecessary pain.

"To this day I have never prayed to be cured of any disease or to allow me to live beyond my permitted time. Both God and Death will only laugh at me if I cannot accept their laws. When others die, I do not think a terrible thing has happened. These are my thoughts on life and death.

"If we see each other again that would be fine. In any case, after some time there will not be any I or you. Instead of waiting for such a day, even now we can merge our separate identities in the One without a Second."

Best Wishes & Blessings
As Ever,
Nitya

41

Leave Takings—I

Some say we are born to serve. I remember an episode of the television program, "The Twilight Zone", when I was a small boy that left a lasting impression upon me. The title of the episode was "To Serve Man." A spacecraft carrying members of a strange civilization landed on Earth. Its crew members were taken captive by the earthlings, while teams of Earth scientists scrutinized the spaceship for secrets of their advanced technology and clues as to the aliens' mission. A book was found that was taken to be the mission manual. After intense examination by linguists, the title of the book was deciphered as "To Serve Mankind." The rest of the book was more difficult to decode.

Convinced of the aliens's good intentions, the earthlings released their captives, and a few adventurous scientists agreed to return with them to their home planet. During the flight one linguist continued his work, and at the end of the show he discovered that "To Serve Mankind" was simply a chapter in a larger book, the title of which was "Inter-Galactic Recipes." Oops!

In Madras this story seems more like history than fantasy. The difference being that the aliens stayed on to colonize the Earth and are known today as "mosquitoes." In Madras one only has to stretch oneself out on a bed, and one immediately has the sensation of becoming the buffet spread at a banquet for the little buggers. Nothing dissuades them. Clothes are little more than place settings. Mosquito repellent seems to be their favorite condiment. And some of them have even learned the art of dive bombing through the swirling current of an electric fan or initiating sneak attacks from whichever side of your body is shielded from the rushing air.

The Madras mosquitoes are so big that they could almost qualify to be the state bird. When they bite, the bite itself hurts in addition to the after-itch. Even Houdini would have to marvel at their ability to get inside a mosquito-net. Somehow the locals have made a kind of peace with them and only seem to notice them when visitors complain of their terrorism. My only consolation was that in two days I would be released from the torture, and when once the swollen marks subsided, I would be able to make light of the ordeal.

The day before yesterday I finished the dictation and editing of the hundred verses and bid farewell to Guru. I have learned the less sentimental I feel when leaving him, the more his presence and teaching have actually percolated into me. Afterall, the true guru is an inner factor of illumination, and attachment to outer forms is contrary to its omnipresence and self-sufficiency.

This time as we said our good-byes, I was uncertain if I would be seeing him again. Given his age, the delicate nature of his health, his insistence on terminating his own world travels, his recent pronouncements on his growing intimacy with death, and of course the unsettledness of my own future, I could only hope we would meet again. Yet my gratitude for my latest opportunity to be with him far outweighed the insecurity about the future.

I was certain that not only the intellectual content of his words, but also the essential beingness of his presence would continue to reverberate within me in the days to come. Each person is like a candle, and the guru is like an ocean of melted wax. Being in the guru's presence is like dipping one's wick in fresh wax, after which one is renewed to light one's own way again.

During my first five or six years with Guru, the image I have of myself is that of a crudely shaped block of granite. At that point Guru acted as a sculptor. A sculptor enters into an inner reciprocity with the stone and chisels off many extraneous and exaggerated formations to create a more beautiful form that was latent within the inner contours of that particular block.

That chipping-off process was often very painful. What may have looked extraneous or exaggerated to the wisdom-eye of the Guru, happened to be some of my own most cherished illusions, prejudices, and habits. Oftentimes the ego was poked in its most sensitive and puffed-up areas. Once when one of his tirades had left me feeling particularly deflated, he gently pointed out that only something which is first inflated is capable of being deflated. His students named this particular aspect of his work "ego-bleaching," and he himself sometimes spoke of the guru's role as being that of a "psycho-surgeon."

Now when I put myself in his presence, I expect to be confronted with my own blind spots and shortcomings. But perhaps Guru is becoming too ripe as he ages, because the last two times I have been with him, he has been consistently sweet from the first to the last. The night before my leaving him, he called me to his bedside and asked me to read out many passages from this journal. He called others around to listen and was generally very supportive. He encouraged me to attempt to publish it.

Anandan came from his office to the railway station to see that my berth reservation was honored. Before the train came, Jyoti and Baby and little Song showed up. Jyoti and Baby were dressed up in my honor and as a treat for them. Song was tear-stained and shaken up, having just been scolded at school by her teacher for having misplaced her lunch box.

Just before leaving for the railway station I had handed Guru a candy bar wrapped in the hundred dollar bill which my eighty year old friend Howard had slipped me back in the U.S. as a contribution to my travel fund. It felt very fine to act as a link between Howard and Guru in this way which neither of them might ever know.

I was reminded of the Native American Indian wisdom

encapsulated in their proverb "The gift must always move," whereby what is received from another is not to be compensated with an in-kind payback to the giver, as is the European economic practice, but rather is to be reciprocated by a gift to an unrelated third party. In this way a disequilibrium is created by which further giving is continually perpetuated; whereas the European practice of direct barter attempts to create an equilibrium or stasis in which one is not to feel indebted or necessarily moved toward further acts of generosity.

A kindred Western expression of this wonderful theory and practice was the suggestion by Herb Caen, columnist for the San Francisco Chronicle, regarding the payment of tolls at the Golden Gate Bridge. Sometimes when he came to the toll gate he would pay his one dollar charge and then give one extra dollar to pay for the unknown driver behind him. His fantasy was that the person behind him would then pay for the person in back of him or her, who would in turn pay for the next person, and so on *ad infinitum*.

The delightful feature of this idea was that after Herb's own small contribution of one dollar, each person would still only be putting out the same dollar that they would otherwise be joylessly paying, except that now each would have the double joy of having been paid for by a stranger on the one hand and paying for a stranger on the other. Although this idea is too mechanical, it does hint at the hidden magic implied in the proverb, "The gift must always move."

I couldn't help but recall another day when I was saying "good-bye" to Guru after a long period of living with him. As I was packing, he walked over and remarked, "You are leaving me this morning. Do you have any doubts you would like cleared up before you go?" "Well," I replied, "I continue to find myself periodically feeling easily irritated with other people. Is there anything I can do to correct that?"

"Oh, that is simply because you are too critical of your mother," was his completely unexpected rejoinder.

My first thought was that maybe he had not understood my question. I had already learned that just because I do not immediately understand something that Guru says does not mean that he is off the mark. "What does that have to do with it?" I inquired.

"Until you feel assured that you have your mother's blessings within you, you will never feel completely at peace with yourself and at ease with others in this lifetime. And of course, if you are not accepting of her, then you will feel a mutual disadoption within yourself. You should think, 'As long as I live, she will always be my mother, and she can do no wrong.'"

It was true that over the years I had become very critical of my mother on many counts, but because the connection between that and a persistent core of irritability (even when I would not see her for months at a time) was so unsuspected, it took me many days to digest what he said.

As it turned out, soon thereafter I made such a resolve as he was suggesting and even declared it to my mother. At first it was only with some effort that I could reverse the habit of judgement and criticism which I had developed with regard to my mother, but within a year I found myself just naturally accepting and appreciative of who she is. Naturally, I found my new attitude was reciprocated both externally and internally. As predicted, my tendency toward impatience and irritability toward others, in general, was also dramatically reduced.

This time as I turned to go, Guru smiled and again asked, "Any questions?" I realized there was something that had been puzzling me about the Indian spiritual teachings. There are said to be two paths to realization and liberation. The first is the path of negation, and the second is the path of affirmation.

In the path of negation, one rejects every specific form and experience as not being the Real, not being God, not being the Self. In practice this means that one constantly repeats to oneself, "Not this. Not this. Not this," with each passing perception, thought and feeling. What remains as a residue after such wholesale negation is said to be It.

In the path of affirmation, one affirms everything one encounters and conceives as being a shining image of the Real, of God, of the Self. "This is It. This is It. This is It." Nothing remains outside Its scope.

I accepted Guru's parting invitation and said, "The path of negation and the path of affirmation seem to contradict each other. Which one is correct? Which should I adopt?"

Guru replied, "It is a disease peculiar to the Western mind to think that things must be either This or That. In the East people think that things are at once 'both this and that' and 'neither this nor that.' Either of these paths, if followed diligently to their conclusion, will lead to the Absolute. Think of it in terms of your self. Either you should think, 'I am nothing, not even this body, mind and senses,' or you should think 'I am everything, including all the people and things that I perceive.'

"Either of these two visions will eventually bring us peace, understanding and unshakable happiness. All our troubles begin only because we mix the two and think, 'I am so

and so but not such and such. This is me, but that is not me.' Don't you see? When all is nothing but the self, there is no self."

THE SELF IS NOWHERE

After a pause Guru spoke again, "I know you well by now. You want to make the world a happier place don't you?"

"Very much, Guru."

"Then maintain yourself as a happy person and add your happiness as a contribution to the collective happiness of all people."

That was a parting gift I recognized that I could always carry with me and which would lighten rather than increase whatever other baggage I might be bearing at the time.

42

Leave Takings—II

The afternoon and overnight train journey to Madras was uneventful. Just as in the Holiday Inn advertisement, on Indian train rides "sometimes the best surprise is no surprise." I was befriended by a young accountant in my compartment, who broke the ice by offering to buy me a cup of tea at one of the stations. I told him I didn't care for any tea, but that I would join him as he went for his. It turned out that he didn't have proper change, and I wound up buying his tea. I noted with pleasure that no big deal was made out of this transactional irony, and we had a nice talk. Later three food service workers noticed me standing at the open door of our coach with my camera and asked to have their picture taken, which I did at the next station. They gave me their address, and I promised to send copies.

At the Madras railway station I bumped into a girl in her early twenties whom I knew from a previous Indian visit eight years back. She is very pretty, but I was most struck by a sadness in her eyes. Surprisingly she responded to my questions with her sad story. She is presently studying for her teaching credential. But in spite of having final exams coming up, she is burdened with all the housework at her home for two months while her mother is visiting an elder sister. She must get up very early each morning, fix breakfast for her father, and then clean up after the meal before rushing off to school. As soon as she gets home in the afternoon, she has housecleaning and clothes washing to take care of before preparing their evening meal. It is already dark, and she is exhausted, yet before she can even begin all of her studying she has to scrub the pots, pans and dishes from dinner.

I commented that she is not only fulfilling her role as a student and daughter but is also expected to do the work of a wife and mother. I noticed her involuntarily flinch and wince when I said "wife." This made me uneasy and suspicious. Later a mutual friend confirmed that her father is not averse to striking her whenever she displeases him. I feared this might not be the only form of abuse.

I was very angry and asked this other friend why the girl herself or someone who knew about this does not report it to the police. "Is beating someone not a crime here?" I pleaded naively.

The response was, "You do not know the system in India. The family is more important than the individual. Even the victim considers the shame that would come upon the family through exposure worse than what she is suffering."

I was quite upset about this. Was this the shadow side of the minimization of personal ego in India? I had to remind myself of how common such abuse has reportedly become in America too. I myself felt the shame.

It was fitting that my last two days in India should be spent with the Kumarans as was my first day. They are like a mother and father to me. Kumaran wanted to know all about the Gurukula Convention, which due to his operation he had missed for the first time in many years. After narrating the flavor and events, I showed him my Inaugural Address, and he eagerly typed himself a copy. His wife, Ammu Etati, had just gotten a small tape recorder and asked me if I would inaugurate it with a message to be played after my departure at the Madras Gurukula's celebration of Nataraja Guru's birth anniversary.

The first afternoon in Madras the Kumarans dropped me in town for some final errands. The first was getting the latch on my cassette player repaired. Indians are the most clever and resourceful repairmen I have ever come across

East or West. I bought some cotton handkerchiefs to take back to Carolyn and a big poster of Ganapati, the elephant-headed god, for teenage Aaron to add to his Punk/Hindu/Buddhist bedroom shrine in California. I bought two books: *The Jaguar Smile; A Nicaraguan Journey* by Salman Rushdie, and a biographical portrait of actress Meryl Streep called *The Reluctant Superstar* to read on my long return journey. I also bought a few medical supplies to round out my first-aid kit and some lightweight hand-woven bath towels.

On my final day in India, I taped some of my reminiscences of Nataraja Guru around the theme of his presentation of Chance with a capital "C" as a good enough modern equivalent for the word "God." I wrote some letters and had a very good time conversing with Suguna. Suguna is a twenty year old nurse who is helping the Kumarans attend on Ammu Etati's aunt who is in a coma.

Long-drawn comas are puzzling phenomena. It looks to me as if the spirit is ambivalently hovering between two states, each with its attractions and threats. On the one hand is life circumlimited to a body with its sensuous enjoyments and social attachments balanced against the infirmities of injury, disease, and old age. And on the other hand is the merger or dissolution into the immortal all-pervasive spirit, the attraction to which is countered by our fear of the unknown.

Suguna is a very outgoing and vivacious young woman with an uncommon boldness to speak her mind. We talked a great deal about cultural differences between America and India, particularly in regard to girl/boy and man/woman relations. But the most eloquent commentary on the subject came when at 5:00 I suggested I would walk her the half kilometer to the bus-stop and send her off. She protested that I "shouldn't go to the trouble." But I insisted that I wanted to. She went to get ready, and five minutes later Ammu Etati approached me as a "go between" to let me know that Suguna would be embarrassed because of what people might say were she to be seen walking with a male.

I would never hold up America as a model for healthy man/woman relations, but in this regard India seems equally out of balance, albeit in the opposite direction. I think as I travel through different cultures, one of the things I am forever on the lookout for is some healthy happy medium in this arena of life.

My last two days in India, I took it as a personal project to drink as many tender coconut waters as possible. It is said that the human body is over 80% water. I wanted at least 50% of that to be coconut juice by the time I left India. My final meal in India consisted of vegetable cutlets (spicy vegiburgers), chapattis, coconut/cabbage curry and *sambar*.

As I boarded the airport coach and turned back to the Kumarans, three hearts melted into a single pool of affection which was sweet beyond regret. Similarly, as the plane rolled down the runway toward lift-off, I reflected how India is more a state of mind than a place in space and time. Hence my silent salutation was not, "So Long," but rather, "Come along."

43

The End As Beginning

From tender coconut juice and fresh tropical fruit salads to canned orange juice from concentrate—it seems Singapore Airlines is trying to make the contrast between the world I am leaving behind and the one toward which I am speeding as clear as possible. The fruit in the fruit salad is as canned as the laughter on many T.V. sitcoms.

Although in an absolute sense our source has nothing to do with national boundaries or societal structures, in a relative sense returning to the U.S.A. is returning to my source. Both my roots and destiny lie in North America. I feel both love and gratitude for the country and its people. Were it not for the American values of personal freedom, technological wizardry, and adventure, I would not have had the interest, gumption, or wherewithal to travel so far from home.

I am returning with a strange blend of contentment and striving, sense of leisure and eagerness. Life is too short and the future too elusive to forego or even postpone one's happiness and the opportunity to share that happiness with others.

Once when Guru was asked if he was happy, he responded, "No, I am not happy. I am Happiness." There is a profound difference between thinking, "I am alive," and knowing, "I am Life." Each of us is that "I am" identified as the Lord in the Biblical declaration, "I am that I am." By definition, whatever is eternal exists right now, and whatever is omnipresent must be right here.

One need not travel to far-flung corners of the world in order to attain the ultimate in terms of self-realization, self-expression and self-fulfillment. There used to be a Native American tradition whereby an apprentice for the position of tribal medicine man underwent a final initiation rite. After a long training in the gathering, preparation and usage of native medicinal herbs, this rite was performed as a test of the student's spiritual preparedness to assume the role of medicine man, which was seen as vital to the well-being of the entire tribe.

Out in the open, the student was brought face to face with his teacher, who then gave his potential successor the assignment of finding, gathering and presenting three wild plants with either nutritional or medicinal value. If the student's first movement was to look down at the ground right around his feet, he was considered to have passed the test and to have proved his preparedness. If, on the other hand, his initial response was to cast a searching glance in the distance or to take a single step in any direction before investigating what was immediately present right where he stood, he was considered to have failed the test.

Upon stepping off the plane which had just returned me to the United States, the first thing I did was gaze down at the ground on which I stood. When I looked up, I could see the very same spirit that I had learned to love in the people of India and had come to recognize as my own self, now mirrored in the faces of all the people I could see in every direction.

ORDER FORM

TEAR OUT & MAIL THIS FORM WITH YOUR CHECK TO:

INNER WEALTH PRESS
P.O. Box 2510-B
Novato, California 94948
(415) 488-0771

Please send me:
___ copies of Mirror By The Road @$12.95 ea. _____
Californians:
    please add $ .85 per book sales tax _____
Shipping:
    $1.50 for 1st book/$.50 each additional book _____

Total Amount Enclosed _____

I understand that I may return any book for a full refund if not satisfied.

Name _____

Address _____

_____ Zip _____

ORDER FORM

TEAR OUT & MAIL THIS FORM WITH YOUR CHECK TO:

INNER WEALTH PRESS
P.O. Box 2510-B
Novato, California 94948
(415) 488-0771

Please send me:
___ copies of Mirror By The Road @$12.95 ea.   _____
Californians:
    please add $ .85 per book sales tax   _____
Shipping:
    $1.50 for 1st book/$.50 each additional book   _____

Total Amount Enclosed   _____

I understand that I may return any book for a full refund if not satisfied.

Name _____

Address _____

        _____ Zip _____